Lewis Turco
and His Work:
A Celebration

IN HONOR OF HIS 70TH BIRTHDAY
MAY 2, 2004

Edited by Steven E. Swerdfeger

Lewis Turco
and His Work:
A Celebration

Copyright © 2004
by Star Cloud Press

cover art by Trisha Hadley

Published by

~ STAR CLOUD PRESS~

an imprint of

Cloudbank Creations, Inc.
6137 East Mescal Street
Scottsdale, Arizona 85254-5418

ISBN: 0-9651835-9-9

Library of Congress Control Number: 2004092631

Printed by Lightning Source
La Vergne, TN

ACKNOWLEDGMENTS

The original, shorter version of *A Garland of Rubliws* was published in an edition limited to 25 copies by the Mathom Bookshop in 1996 (all rights reserved) and distributed as a thank-you gift to all those who had participated in or contributed to the retirement banquet of Lewis Turco. After this distribution, rubliws continued to be written and published, and many of those are included here.

"Whole Meaning Again" by Herbert R. Coursen, Jr., is from the "Introduction" to *American Still Lifes*, Oswego: The Mathom Publishing Company, 1981; "A Certain Slant of Light: The Poetry of Lewis Turco" in *Companion to Contemporary American Literature* from the Editors of *The Hollins Critic*, ed. R. H. W. Dillard and Amanda Cockrell, Farmington Hills: Twayne Publishers, 2002, and from "The Ghosts of Blinn's Hill," the foreword to *The Green Maces of Autumn, Voices in an Old Maine House*, Dresden Mills: The Mathom Bookshop, 2002.

"A Poetics of the Psyche" by Mary Doll is from the *Dictionary of Literary Biography: Yearbook 1984*, ed. Jean W. Ross, Detroit: Gale Research, 1985, pp. 331-338.

"The Progress of Lewis Turco" by William Heyen is from *Modern Poetry Studies*, ii:3, 1971, pp. 115-24.

"Foreword" by Donald Justice is from *First Poems* by Lewis Turco, Francestown: Golden Quill Press, 1960.

"Making the Language Dance and Go Deep" by Donald Masterson appeared in *The Cream City Review* of the University of Wisconsin — Milwaukee, vol. 8, nos. 1-2, 1983.

"The Mirror Image: A Retrospective View of Lewis Turco" by De Villo Sloan is from "A Capacity for Song" in *The Sewanee Review*, xcix:4, Fall 1991, and from Voices in Italian Americana, iii:1, Spring 1992.

"Singing to the Same Tune, but with Different Words" by Felix Stefanile is from a review in *Italian Americana*, i:2, Spring 1975, and from the "Preface" to *A Book of Fears*, West Lafayette: Bordighera, 1998, winner of the first annual Bordighera Bilingual Poetry Prize.

"Terra Imaginaria" by Gene Van Troyer was compiled from reviews in *Star * Line*, v:1, Jan.-Feb. 1982; v:4, Jul.-Aug. 1982, vii:1, Jan.-Feb. 1984, and from an essay of the same title in *The English Record*, xlii:2, 1992.

"Sharing the Path or Circuit of Things through Forms," by Hyatt H. Waggoner is a conflation of an essay, "The Formalism of Lewis Turco: Fluting and Fifing with Frosted Fingers," originally published in *Concerning Poetry*, ii:2, Fall 1969, and a review published in The Hollins Critic, xxiii:5, December 1986.

"The Anachronist" by Gerhard Zeller appeared in *E.L.F.: Eclectic Literary Forum*, viii:1, Spring 1998.

CONTENTS

Additional Poems & Tributes

* * * *

for

LEWIS TURCO

*in grateful appreciation
for his enduring contributions
to American Letters and Scholarship*

WHO WAS THAT MASKED MAN?
AMERICAN POETRY'S DEBT OF GRATITUDE
TO LEWIS TURCO
R. S. Gwynn

WE ARE GATHERED THIS EVENING [October 18, 1996] to honor
Lewis Turco on the occasion of his retirement from teaching, and I am
going to attempt to offer some propositions about what his career has
meant, both to me personally and to American poetry in general. I will
speak personally first, for in requesting that I give this talk Lew Turco
has honored me as well, and I am pleased tonight to return one of many
favors he has done me over the years. I won't go into the exact nature
of those favors because if Lew totaled them up he might send me a bill
for services rendered. I first met Lew at the Bread Loaf Writers Conference in the summer of 1968. We immediately established that we
had something in common: neither of us liked my poems very much.
He did, however, encourage me to keep writing in hopes that I would
eventually produce something that both of us could live with. It means
a lot for an undergraduate poet to get encouragement at an early stage
of the career, and Lew offered it. I trust that he has been offering similar
encouragement to younger poets in the ensuing years.

At the outset, I must frankly say that I find the whole notion of
Lewis Turco retiring fairly absurd; anyone who knows Lew at all will
know that comparisons between his energy level and that of a perpetual
motion machine will find the machine in distant second place. He will
no longer teach, true, but he will continue to write poetry and criticism,
and even while tending store in his Mathom Bookshop in Maine he will
probably still find plenty to be contentious about when he surveys the
current poetry scene. I have recently edited an anthology of the works
of early modernist American poet-critics called *The Advocates of Poetry*.

1

That is what Lew Turco is — an advocate of poetry, one who is unafraid to speak out when he feels that the art form he loves so well is threatened. There have been many threats to the health and well-being of American poetry over the last few decades, and Lew Turco has seen them clearly and has spoken out most consistently against that self-centered school of contemporary poetry he labels "egopoetics." The positions he has taken have rarely been popular, but the time has now come when the stances he has favored for over thirty years are once again respectable and may even prevail. As Ralph Waldo Emerson, one of the many writers with whom Lew has had a long and contentious relationship, said: "If the single man plant himself indomitably on his instincts, and there abide, the huge world will come round to him." That is what Lew Turco has done, and the huge world is finally coming round to him. The title of my talk is, "Who Was That Masked Man? American Poetry's Debt of Gratitude to Lewis Turco." I suspect that most of us over what the French would call "un certain âge" will have no trouble with the question raised by my title, "Who Was That Masked Man?"; younger members of the audience, though, may be mystified. The Masked Man I refer to was, of course, the famous Lone Ranger, whose radio and television shows were announced each week by the stirring tones of the William Tell Overture and a hearty "Hi-Yo, Silver! "Like most media heroes of the distant past, the Lone Ranger was a good man. He did good and spoke good. His faithful Indian companion or kemo-sabe, Tonto, also did good but didn't speak so good. Usually an episode of The Lone Ranger concerned a group of oppressed persons, usually speaking with Swedish accents, who were being oppressed by large men with even larger mustaches. The Lone Ranger would ride into town on his white stallion Silver, right wrongs by punching a few large men with even larger mustaches, and then ride off into the sunset without waiting for the grateful and no longer oppressed farmers to thank him. His identity remained obscure. Each episode ended with someone, usually an innocent maiden with a

Swedish accent, asking, "Who vas dot masked man, ja?" The answer was always the same: "Why, I don't know, ja."

I have a clue to the identity of the Lone Ranger. I believe that he is with us tonight. True, he did not ride into Oswego on a raging white stallion, but anyone who has driven with him for more than a couple of blocks will attest that he does not go in fear of trifles like stop signs or speed limits. I do not know who was oppressing the student-writers of SUNY-Oswego before his coming, but I do know that these writers have prospered during his tenure here and that he leaves behind him, as he gallops off into the sunset, a writing arts program that is one of the strongest in the nation. True, he does not have a faithful Indian companion whose name, Tonto, means "Foolish," but he does have me to serve as his kemo-sabe for the evening. While I have no Native American blood, I have shed quite a bit of my own at various gambling establishments from Santa Fe, New Mexico, to Coushata, Louisiana, to Mohawk, New York, and it may be that the Lone Ranger will leave tonight without our having thanked him sufficiently for all that he has done for us. This Masked Man is hanging up his academic spurs and placing his trusty six-shooter, loaded, one supposes, with red ink, in its holster for good. So as we watch him fade away into the sunset, one of us may well ask, "Who, indeed, was that masked man?"

Well, we all know who he was, and is. Lew Turco is the masked man, and that would seem to answer all the questions about his identity. But would it? When we speak of William Butler Yeats, we invoke the title of one of Richard Ellmann's critical books on the great Irishman, *The Man and the Masks*. When we speak of Lewis Turco's various personae, we should also recall that that Greek word means masks as well. So which of Lew Turco's masks should we talk about? Do we mean Professor Turco, distinguished college teacher and administrator? Or do we mean Lewis Putnam Turco, the award-winning literary critic? Or do we mean one of his many other guises: Pocoangelini, the tragi-comic Italian Everyman? Or the nameless "Inhabitant" of another sequence of poems? Or Lewis Turco-Burton,

3

The Compleat Melancholick? Or the Belle of Amherst's alter-ego, Emilew Dickinson? Or Wesli Court, the anagrammatic rhyming jester? Or do we simply mean plain Lewis Turco, American poet? A brief survey of the many masks of Lewis Turco is perhaps the only way of comprehending the singular individual behind them.

To be sure, Lew Turco came by his personal identity crisis honestly. First, his ancestry is Italian. It is a great mystery that Italy should be the homeland of Virgil, Petrarch, and Dante, but that relatively few Italian-Americans have become poets. This great literary heritage, when transplanted to what has otherwise proven friendly soil, has not prospered proportionately, and, along with Lew himself, Italian-American writers like Gay Talese have pondered why. Reading the selected letters of Lew's mentor, the late John Ciardi, I find this passage, addressed to Lew: "Lew Turco is an American poet who happens to have Italian parents. If the human race could not somehow have managed to evade its parents we'd all be federal bureaucrats."

But Ciardi was Italian, too, and no one talks about the masks of John Ciardi, a man who, I can tell you from personal experience, wouldn't have given an identity crisis the time of day. Lew, however, managed to compound the problem by being not just Italian but also a Baptist, and not just a Baptist but a Baptist of the nth degree, what we in the South used to refer to as a P.K., or preacher's kid. In an early poem he writes of his father:

AN IMMIGRANT BALLAD

My father came from Sicily
   (O sing a roundelay with me)
With cheeses in his pocket and
A crust of black bread in his hand.
He jumped ashore without a coat,
   Without a friend or enemy,
Till Jesus nailed him by the throat.

My father came to Boston town
 (O tongue a catch and toss one down).
By day he plied a cobbler's awl,
By night he loitered on the mall.
He swigged his wine, he struck his note,
 He wound the town up good and brown,
Till Jesus caught him by the throat.

He'd heard of Hell, he knew of sin
 (O pluck that wicked mandolin),
But they were for the gentle folk,
The cattle broken to the yoke.
He didn't need a Cross to tote:
 His eyes were flame, his ears were tin,
Till Jesus nabbed him by the throat.

He met a Yankee girl one day
 (O cry a merry roundelay)
Who wouldn't do as she was bid,
But only what the good folk did.
She showed him how the church bells peal
 Upon the narrow straitaway,
And Jesus nipped him by the heel.

My father heard a sermon said
 (O bite the bottle till it's dead).
He quit his job and went to school
And memorized the Golden Rule.
He drained his crock and sold his keg,
 He swept the cobwebs from his head,
And Jesus hugged him by the leg.

The girl was pleased: she'd saved a soul
    (O light a stogie with a coal).
No longer need she be so wary:
Daddy went to seminary
To find how warm a Yankee grows
    When she achieves her fondest goal.
And Jesus bit him on the nose.

At last he had a frock to wear
    (O hum a hymn and lip a prayer).
He hoisted Bible, sailed to search
For sheep to shear and for a church.
He asked the girl to share his life,
    His choir-stall and shirt of hair,
For Jesus bade him take a wife.

My father holds a pulpit still
    (O I have had enough to swill).
His eye is tame, his hair is gray,
He can't recall a roundelay.
But he can preach, and he can quote
    A verse or scripture, as you will,
Since Jesus took him by the throat.

When you put these ingredients together in the fashion of our present multicultural times, you come up with "Italian-American Baptist Poet." It is an interesting label, to be sure, but also a rather unlikely one.

    But that's not all. In a companion piece to the poem which I just quoted, "Requiem for a Name," Lew speaks of his mother's side of the family:

REQUIEM FOR A NAME

Believe it or believe it not,
      My mother was a Putnam once.
  On her ancestral tree she swears
The Lowells and the Deweys too
    Hang pendulous as lovely pears.
      My grampaw was a sort of dunce
Who rather let things go to pot —

Himself, his offspring, farm and wife.
      My grampaw was a sort of dunce.
  His homestead I remember well:
The floors were warped, the doors askew,
    And now and then the rafters fell.
      My mother was a Putnam once —
She led a less than social life,

So she went East from grampaw's West.
      My mother was a Putnam once
    Till she was married, woe O! woe.
No longer was she maiden free —
    She cursed her pa from pate to toe.
      My grampaw was a sort of dunce
To cheat the eaglet in its nest

By willing her a woman's form.
      My grampaw was a sort of dunce,
    But what a hefty name he wore!
He gave my middle name to me;
    It fits me like a saddlesore.
      My mother was a Putnam once,
I'd be one too, come sun or storm.

7

The Deweys and the Lowell hosts
Are pendant from a hollow tree.
Now with this rime let them be felled,
Let me be nothing more to me
Than windfalls blasted by the frosts.

My mother was a Putnam once;
My grampaw was a sort of dunce.

Putnam. The very name reverberates with the high-toned genealogies of purest New England. It has been said that in old Boston the Lowells spoke only to the Cabots and the Cabots spoke only to God. Rumor has it that the Putnams considered their own station so lofty that they spoke only to themselves, and even then somewhat condescendingly. Add a dash of Putnam to that Sicilian Turco sauce, and you have a rather unusual entree to bring to the Baptist covered-dish supper.

Given such beginnings, what, then, is such a bright young man from Meriden, Connecticut, to do about answering the eternal question, "Who am I?" A century or so earlier, a bright young man from Long Island with a similarly conflicted family background answered it by proclaiming himself a "kosmos" — "Turbulent, fleshly, sensual, eating, drinking and breeding, / No sentimentalist, no stander above men and women or apart from them, / No more modest than immodest," finding in the "scent of these armpits aroma finer than prayer." I can't speak for what kind of scent the young Lew Turco found in his own armpits, but it certainly wasn't Eau de Walt Whitman. A high-school visit to New York City, as he tells us in an essay titled "Whitman and I" [in *The Public Poet, Five Lectures on the Art and Craft of Poetry*, 1991] impressed him less with the Good Gray Poet's prophetic vision of "Mannahatta" than with the filth, grime, and human wreckage of those mean streets. As he says, "My negative response to Whitman was as formative for me as a positive response has been for another writer." The person whom he describes as "the minister's son in his adolescent disillusionment" returned from the field trip and wrote a long poem called "The City's Masque" (please note the title, fellow deconstructionists!), which brought him his first poetic honors. He knew that he would not find his own identity as a poet by losing himself in a grubby urban rite of passage. Lew Turco did not cross Brooklyn Ferry; instead, he joined the Navy. Thus, before he was twenty, he had already worn two masks, that of Lewis Turco, Boy Wonder Poet, and that of Yeoman Third Class Turco, who credits the Navy with first teaching him to type and then giving him plenty of leisure time between filling out triplicate forms to practice the rudiments of his poetic craft. When he returned to civilian life Lew would get plenty of opportunities to practice those rudiments, first at the University of Connecticut and later at the graduate workshop of the University of Iowa. By the time he was twenty-six he had published his first book and had begun a successful teaching career. Enough on the subject of humble beginnings.

I should first speak of the professorial mask, but it is that aspect of Lew Turco's career that I am least equipped to talk about. I do know that Lew is a master teacher, a fact that was impressed upon me the first time I heard him lecture, at the Bread Loaf Writer's Conference in the summer of 1968. While Lew was holding forth eloquently on the twin evils of free verse and deep images, he was attacked by an irate chipmunk whose behavior obviously marked him as a devoted partisan of the poetry of Robert Bly. That Lew managed to hold on to his composure, as well as the attention of his audience, was, I thought, a major accomplishment. At the time I was considering a teaching career myself, and I filed away Lew's example of courage under fire in a chipmunk-proof mental drawer. Some twenty-five years later, I visited one of Lew's classes here, and I was happy to watch him keep the attention of his students under somewhat less trying circumstances. His textbook *Poetry: An Introduction through Writing* [1973] has long been one of the most useful books on my shelf, and his remarks to Alberta

9

Turner in the book *Poets Teaching: The Creative Process*, [Longman, 1980] should be considered by anyone entering the profession.

The best measure of Lew's success, though, is the state of health of the Writing Arts program here. It has grown under his care to become one of the most admired and widely imitated programs in the United States, and the later careers of its graduates have been impressive, to say the least. And Lew cannot be accused of not putting his money where his mouth is or, to put it more accurately, of not putting his money where his daughter is: his daughter Melora is an honor graduate of the Writing Arts program. I wonder how many of us in education would entrust our own children to a program that we were responsible for designing. So we have removed one more mask. Another of Lew's early poems turns on the refrain: "At least the old professor is employed." In his case, I would alter it to read, "Thank god the old professor has been employed — here."

Now to look at another mask: Lewis Putnam Turco, literary critic. It is easier to speak of this side of Lew's career, for the literary world perhaps best knows Lew for his criticism. A decade ago, his collection of essays *Visions and Revisions of American Poetry* [1986] won the Melville Cane Award from the Poetry Society of America. I would recommend this book to any young poet who finds him- or herself dismayed by the prevailing notion that American poetry sprang fully armed from the furrowed brows of a two-headed monster named Ralph Waldo Whitman. *Visions and Revisions* offers a parallel history of American poetry, one which begins with what Lew calls our first "professional" poets — Anne Bradstreet and Phyllis Wheatley — and extends to the present day with poets who are less concerned with using poetry to achieve mystical visions or to explore a theory than with using it to entertain and enlighten the reader. Lew's views on the poetic profession always favor the poet who is a professional, i.e., one who is content to be a poet and not a guru or theorist.

But it is for two other critical books that Lew Turco most earns our respect and gratitude. I am speaking, of course, of *The Book of Forms: A*

Handbook of Poetics [1968] and of *The New Book of Forms* [1986]. I can best explain the impact of *The Book of Forms* and its successor by explaining what they have meant to me as a practicing poet. When I began to write as an undergraduate, the prevailing mode in American poetry was free verse, a term Lew despises less for what it represents than, characteristic for him, for its sheer oxymoronic inaccuracy. If a young poet submitted a sonnet to a leading literary magazine, he or she was more likely than not to receive a curt note suggesting that meter and rhyme went out with fender skirts and bobby sox and that the young poet should, in the parlance of the times, tune in, turn on, get groovy, etc., by learning how to express him- or herself in a less coherent manner. During that time, the existence of *The Book of Forms* was about the only evidence that a formal tradition existed in American poetry. It was only years later that I learned that I was not alone in burning the midnight oil trying to work out the intricacies of the rhupunt; the cyrch a chwta (kirch a choo-tah); the favorite form of the Reagan era, the rannaigheact (ronnie-act), or my personal favorite, rimas dissolutas, which are guaranteed to turn any poet who attempts them dissolute. There were obviously other masochists among my generation, for today there is a thriving movement in American poetry called the New Formalism, a movement that Lew anticipated a dozen years ago when he began to write about "neo-formalism" in American poetry ["The Year in Poetry," *Dictionary of Literary Biography Yearbook of American Poetry*, 1983-86]. Today there are several respected journals like *Sparrow* and *The Formalist* that are devoted to poetry in traditional forms, and even a mainstream quarterly like *The Hudson Review* has become more and more receptive to metrical poetry. There are critical books and new anthologies like the one I hold in my hand, *The Rebel Angels: Twenty-Five Poets of the New Formalism*, that all attest to the health of a thriving literary movement. The poets who are part of it know whom to thank. Here are a few of their words about *The Book of Forms* and its author.

This comes from Annie Finch, who has edited *A Formal Feeling Comes*, an anthology of formalist poetry by American women poets: "This radically eclectic and refreshingly inclusive handbook breathed new energy and imagination into poetics at a time when they were most needed." And this from Timothy Steele, one of the leading new formalist poets whose critical book *Missing Measures* explains the cultural and aesthetic reasons behind the decision of modern poets to abandon meter and form: "When I was a student, trying to learn about the art of poetry, most of the texts that I consulted spoke unhelpfully of voice and vision. What a pleasure it was to discover Lewis Turco's *Book of Forms*, which offered sensible and sensitive discussions of verse technique. The book was and remains a model of its kind." And here is David Mason, co-editor with Mark Jarman of *The Rebel Angels*: "Whatever the New Formalism means for American poetry today, it would simply not have happened without the steadfast acknowledgment by Lewis Turco...that measured speech could still be vital. At a time when rhyme and meter were actively discouraged among younger writers...many of us began to write in isolation and with little sense of what direction we might take; for that reason, *The Book of Forms* became an essential text, a kind of road map to the possible." These and similar sentiments have also been spoken to me lately by many other poets, who represent a diverse cross-section of American poetry: among them are Robert Phillips, William Matthews, Marilyn Hacker, and Dana Gioia. And he also has the thanks of an older generation of American poets as well. When I asked Richard Wilbur, the poet whom almost every New Formalist credits as an important influence, to contribute a few words to this talk, he was happy to respond with a poem in a new verse form:

FOR LEWIS TURCO
Dear Lew,
All hail to you.
Old formalist, who through

Your *Book of Forms* inform the new.
If you can name this bloody form, please do
Before it disappears from view,
For you're the one man who
Might manage to.
Adieu.

[For Lew's response, see "A Garland of Rubliws," below.]

Well, for once the masked man has stuck around long enough to receive the thanks of those whom he has helped. As much as I hate the jargon of touchy-feely, I must say that Lew "was there for us" during a period when precious few other poets and critics were.

Here is what his publisher Miller Williams, director of the University of Arkansas Press, has to say: "I met Lew Turco and Robert Frost at the same time, at the Bread Loaf Writers Conference in 1962. Impressed as I was to be in the presence of Frost, I was just about as impressed to learn that Lew had had the nerve to go by the great poet's home on the way there, speak to him, and leave his own poems. As the years passed and I became increasingly glad to call Lew a friend, I became increasingly aware that timidity would never be much of a bother to him, and that's a blessing for all of us. Maybe it's not a totally unalloyed blessing, given that the natural force of his personality has allowed him to coin puns that many would be afraid to let loose from their lips, but that same presence let him stand undaunted through years of almost single-handed battle for balance and good sense in poetry and poetics."

Here are some words from poet and critic X. J. Kennedy: "I know of no poet whose command of forms and measures is stronger or wider than Lew's. A Turco poem is, to say the least, always technically interesting and splendidly well made. For all this while, Lew has kept an unwavering devotion to the highest standards of his craft. Is it necessary to add that, besides, his poems have much to tell us, and that, like Lew himself, they abound in deep and powerful and sometimes delicate feelings? He has long been one of the indispensable great forces for good in our poetry, and I heartily wish him well for now and always."

I come now to the final part of my talk, a few words about the last of the masks, that of Lewis Turco, American poet. How do you attempt to sum up a forty-year career while it's still in progress? You don't. My suggestion, which I am sure Lew would second, is for everyone here tonight to rush out and buy *The Shifting Web* [1989], Lew's volume of new and selected poems, and read through it, as I did the other night for the umpteenth time. You can make your own conclusions. But if you're not disposed to do so, let me offer a few for you to make. One is obvious: Lew Turco is a poet of many paradoxes. The first of these is that this most sociable of creatures should, among earlier American poets, so completely identify with the reclusive Emily Dickinson that he has written, or perhaps "found" is the better word, a whole sequence of poems based on passages from her correspondence, "A Sampler of Hours: Poems and Centos from Lines in Emily Dickinson's Letters" [in *Emily Dickinson, Woman of Letters*, 1993]. The connection with Ms. Dickinson is made more clear, however, if you have ever visited the attic room where Lew has worked on his poems over the years. I am not suggesting that Lew frequents the upper stories of his house while wearing a white dress and bundling up his poems in pink ribbons (only Jean would know the truth of that) but simply that, in a devotion to craft to the exclusion of whatever emperor might be kneeling on his mat, his soul has certainly selected its own society in a manner worthy of Emily Dickinson. He may not be the Belle of Amherst, but he is certainly the Beau of Oswego. Here is one of my favorite poems of Lew's:

ATTIC POEM

This is already old. When you find these pages
they will be brown as autumn. The ink
will look like bottled shadow etched
on a leaf. The attic room in which I write

will stand in these words only, if it stands, if it
ever stood. I see myself as I am now
as through an hourglass telescope reversed,
the falling sand turning the sight grainy

as a curled photograph: The man writes
in his house by the lake, in rainy weather,
his family asleep below — the two crones
and the ancient boy, his trucks scaled to rust.

That love is dead; all the trees are leaving.
It is spring, it is the fifth spring
since I was that other
not dreaming of a son:

It was as though he were a hollow fang
filled with midwinter and night. The bed was sweaty.
The ache was solid, without a sharp center.
He marveled that so much pain could keep him alive.

Sand is filling the attic room.
Leaves are turning in the night.
That love is dead, twice dead.
Darken it now. Close the book.

I can only speculate on the reasons why such a "public poet," as Lew has termed himself in a series of essays, should so resolutely seek privacy, but I suspect it has something to do with a side of our personalities that most poets, especially male poets, rarely reveal: the capacity for being wounded, even when the facade of books and reputation would seemingly render the poet most invulnerable. One of Lew's alter egos, Pocoangelini, puts it this way:

POCOANGELINI 38

"You have many wrinkles,"
Pocoangelini told the mirror.
But my wrinkles are of glass, the mirror
replied. "And your hands, Mr. Glass, look like
    the talons of a bird."

    That is true, the mirror
said, but my hands are made of glass. It smiled
at Pocoangelini. "Yet glass can
wither too," Pocoangelini said.
    "My heart is a glass heart:

    "in it a crystal world
spins out its hours in little figures. Snow
falls when one tilts it. Bright fish swim among
coral clouds. Glass can wither," Poco said.
    "My heart is a glass heart."

Second, while Lew is truly a genius in employing the many forms of poetry, he has chosen, in his selected poems, to let other aspects of his work come to the fore. You will search *The Shifting Web* in vain for villanelles, sestinas, or any of the more elaborate fauna of *The Book of Forms*. You won't even find such familiar forms as the sonnet. Instead, you will encounter some rhyme, some blank verse, a great deal of syllabic poetry, and even a prose poem or two. Why this exclusion? One answer is simple enough: Lew has invented a stand-in, one Wesli Court, to write the poetry of formal brilliance while Lewis Turco prefers to wear the plain clothes of less obvious examples of formal control.

This comes from the poet who has probably known Lew the longest, Donald Justice, his former teacher at Iowa and his longtime friend: "Writing has always been as natural for Lew as walking or, for that matter, amusing his friends. He improvised an alter ego, Wesli Court, to take care of the overflow of Turco poems. Whenever I see in a magazine now a certain kind of poem — one witty and formally inventive and perhaps light-hearted, with verve and fizz and a few surprises — and if this poem is signed by a name unfamiliar to me, I tend to suspect that I may be reading the work of still another Turco spin-off. How many Turcos there really are I shall probably never know, but a whole townful would be all right with me." Don Justice also provides me with a bit of information that I wasn't aware of before: "When Lew was in graduate school," Justice tells us, "he was the champion of two parlor tricks for which alone we would never have forgotten him, even if he had written nothing: one was the trick of being able to recite anything backwards, and to do it instantly; the second and more impressive was the trick of improvising on the spot a Dylan Thomas poem, not ever one we could quite remember, though each new Turco-Thomas poem did sound at least faintly familiar and certainly authentic."

But I believe there is a deeper reason as well. It has something to do with another strange paradox, that Lew Turco, whom none would accuse of hiding his candle under a bushel basket, is fundamentally a modest man. Over and over, these poems seem to be saying, "Judge us on our depths, not our surfaces." Perhaps this is the result of having lived and taught within sight of Lake Ontario; a poet can't live and work close to water without its becoming a controlling metaphor.

Whatever the surface of the lake reveals, one who has learned to read the water knows that the mystery lies below.

My third and final point is related to the other two. As I have noted, Lew Turco's poetry is largely one of exclusions and absences. By exclusions I mean his desire not to show off his technical skill at every turn; by absences I mean the remarkable scarcity of first person pronouns in his work. Just to test a theory, I made a count and came up with a total of fewer than 200 instances of "I" in *The Shifting Web*. When we consider that many of the I's that do appear belong to personae other than himself, the total is remarkable, perhaps the smallest in any collection of selected poems by a living poet. Lew has consistently refused to follow the crowd in his career, but the most important grain that he has gone against is the confessional one. In an American poetry that has increasingly come to resemble not so much *Masterpiece Theater* as Geraldo, Lewis Turco has declined to flagellate his wife, his loved ones, and himself on the printed page:

LETTER TO W. D. S[nodgrass]

Christ, you made me sad
with your love tunes gone awry,
the bitter root twining mossily
among the pages of a songsheet tossed to

wind down the wind and
moulder in a lost cranny
of some meadow. I'm not used to loss,
though aware of it, as one is aware of

cancer. A woman
I knew, wrinkled like blown snow,
died of a wild part of herself which
ravened its own life. Her children, grown to seed

themselves, kept locks on
their tongues, but their hearts' faceless
prisoner snarled at the world behind
portcullises of eyes. Like those striped lines of

yours, that scourge of ink
and pillory of paper.
Why did you flay yourself there, in the
marketplace? Was it because sorrow shown is

simpler than covert
loneliness? All of us are
alone. The world we blow through is cold.
Snow fetters our sorrow. Still we flute and fife.

Which is not to say that he is an impersonal poet. What did Marianne Moore once say about such a poetry of exclusion? It is in her poem "Silence": "The deepest feeling always shows itself in silence; / Not in silence but restraint." I believe that Lewis Turco's poetry does this as well. Here is "Poem," the last piece in Lew's selected poems:

POEM

It is time to write a poem.
You have spun out the string of hours —
it winds down the road, across
people's lawns; it tangles itself
in the bushes of the park, catches
in the lower limbs of a horse

chestnut, and there, now, it lifts to
a kite, a blue kite against the gray
sky. You must shinny after

it. When you've caught it, hauled it down
by its rag tail, you see your poem
    scrawled on the tissue wrinkling in

    your hand.   You feel the balsa rib
bow. Windcaught, the kite whispers free, sweeps
    across the street, blowing like
    the spiders that ride the air as
voyagers: you have read that somewhere;
    the kite spins out its line. You can

    not now follow. Your hands stop. No
longer do they climb and circle. You
    have seen the poem. The day
    freezes in its frame. The words squirm
out from beneath your hand. The wind is
    solid air, the clouds the color

    of waiting. Only the kite moves
above the still neighbors in their rooms,
    on their lawns, amid their sounds
    turned to rosedust hovering in
a blank white square of world: When that is
    done, things will move again. The kite

    will be somewhere in the center
of the shifting web it is weaving.
    You will follow it, follow
    the filament from pause to pause,
poem to poem. It is almost
    done. You can feel the wind stirring.

As we follow the filaments of meaning from pause to pause, poem to
poem, we begin to grasp what a rare treasure these poems comprise, and
in that discovery we honor their maker.

With that in mind, let me conclude with my own tribute, a rare example of a form that Lew can add to the next edition of *The Book of Forms*. It is known as the assbackwards Dylanic. I've titled it,

ELLENALLIV FOR LEW: ON HIS RETIREMENT

Retirement into gentle go not do.
Dies he until stops never poet a.
Do to tasks undone many have still you.

Start they what of half finish ever few.
You with compared they're when away fade they.
Retirement into gentle go not do.

Renown first their on rested have some, true.
Promises early to up live few, hey!
Do to tasks undone many have still you.

Writes who man the to given be must due
Does he what for reward small too is pay
Retirement into gentle go not do.

Yield to not and, find to, seek to, strive to.
Truth its holds still saw ancient this that pray
Do to tasks undone many have still you.

Sleep you before go to miles have you, Lew
Forth travel you may so, anew breaks day.
Retirement into gentle go not do.
Do to tasks undone many have still you.

Who is this masked man, indeed? And how shall we thank him? I suggest that we start by giving him a warm round of applause and asking him to say a few words for himself.

A GARLAND OF RUBLIWS

on the Retirement from the Groves of Academe
of LEWIS TURCO

FOR RICHARD WILBUR[1]

> Dear Dick,
> It's quite a trick
> To name the form poetic
> You sent Sam Gwynn who, in the nick
> Of time, included it in his panegyric
> Celebrating my arthritic
> Remove from the academic,
> But rubliw's a quick
> Kick.

> Lew Turco

RUBLIW FOR DONALD JUSTICE

> Dear Don,
> I came upon
> This brand new form quite hon-
> estly the other day, whereon
> It sort of turned into an antiphon,
> If not a kind of poetic icon
> Found in no lexicon,
> But it shall anon,
> Hereon.

> Lew Turco

RUBLIW FOR DANA GIOIA

Dear Dan—
a, in the main,
A rubliw is a skein
Of monorhymes making a chain
To this point that's formally a cinquain,
But then the lines, like a train
Losing cars, refrain
And start to wane
Again.

Lew Turco

RUBLIW FOR DAVID MASON

Dear Dave,
At our conclave
The other day a stave
One line longer than an octave
Given in by Wilbur made a slave
Of me, and I must now behave
As though I were a knave.
I seek my grave!
I rave!

Lew Turco

A NOTE TO LEWIS TURCO[2]

Dear Lew,
Although it's true
Apologies are due,
I hope you'll never misconstrue
Silence as disregard. Before I'm through
Or turn blue trying to out-do
The likes of you-know who,
One overdue
Thank you.

But Gott!
We're in a spot
Since Mark and I forgot
Your *Book of Forms* when we begot
Our *Rebel Angels*. Some mistakes we caught
In time, but others leave us fraught
And bothered, like dry-rot.
We'll rue the blot
A lot.

David Mason

P.S.
The verse-duress
Of Rubliws causes stress
And worse — long nights of sleeplessness
In which I hear the same rhymes to excess.
I have prayed God would repossess
My brain. My lawyer, Wes,
Has your address....
Confess!

LETTER TO *THE FORMALIST*[3]

Dear Bill:
I've had my fill
Of rubliw overkill.
Resilient rhyming makes me ill
(and somewhat shrill) so I'll abstain until
You beg for more from Evansville —
Which I don't think you will
Because my skill
Is nil.

A guy
Who can't deny
That something went awry
Should have a better alibi
Than Mason, who was forced to versify
Where rebel angels fear to fly
Until his whole supply
Of humble pie
Ran dry.

It's not
That I won't squat
To take the cheapest shot
Or will not stoop to polyglot.
It's just these rubliws tie me in a knot
Of chiming rhymes. I've tried to jot
Some lines you'd like a lot
But what I've got
Is rot.

To say
More may convey
A sense I am blasé
About these grinding rhymes. No way!
I'll send you sonnets, a stray virelai
Or my risqué roman â clef
But rubliws are passé.
Yours truly, A.
M. J.

A. M. Juster

RUBLIW FOR R. S. GWYNN

Dear Sam,
That big grand slam
You hammered out I am
As grateful for as an unsteamed clam
At a lobster feed would be, ad nauseam.
This rubliw comes from the diaphragm
At the very least. My RAM
Is about to jam —
I'll scram.

Lew Turco

RUBLIW FOR LOEU

Dear Loeu,
I doeu hope yoeu
Will very soeun be throeu
With this roeud form of clerihoeu

And, troeuly, take a vow that yoeu'll eschoeu
All stoeupid verse forms that are noeu
Of which foeu should accroeu
Within your oeu-
vre, toeu.

Sam Gwynn

RUBLIW FOR X. J. KENNEDY

Dear Joe,
Sam Gwynn's show
The other night was so
Gung-ho it left an afterglow
Of great good will. I wanted you to know
I'm conscious of how much I owe
You for your apropos
And bright bon mot
Rainbow.

Lew Turco

RUBLIW FOR LEW TURCO

Dear Lew,
Whattaya bet that few
Poets of dernier cri or premier cru,
Given the chance, would modestly name a new
Form for Dick Wilbur (not ocrut or ydennek)? Screw
Such glory-grabbers! Lord, they make me spew —
You're rare as a good old golden yew.
See you in *Rubliw*
Review.

Joe Kennedy

RUBLIW FOR TIMOTHY STEELE

Dear Tim,
Please let me limn,
E'er passing time bedim
The mem'ry of Sam's banquet hymn,
My gratitude for your good paradigm
Of kindness. It filled my cup to the rim —
Up to the very brim —
And there I swim
With vim.

Lew Turco

RUBLIW FOR MILLER WILLIAMS

Dear Miller,
You are a pillar
Of poesy, distiller
Of lore, a gentleman instiller
Of great goodwill. My thanks to you, thou swiller
Of the Empyrean vanilla
Shake — (oops! that's a killer,
A Down-East filler,
Feller).

Lew Turco

RUBLIW FOR SHARON VAN SLUIJS

Dear Sharon,
Thanks for baring
Your talent and for sharing
It with me...with us. Airing
Poems at a marathon is wearing,
To say the least, but it's not daring
For me to be swearing
You all were raring,
Not barren.

Lew Turco

RUBLIW FOR MAXINE KUMIN

Maxine,
You were the queen
Who lent her shine and sheen
Unto Oswego's dim demesne
The other day. Thanks for your careen
From bard to verse. With sweet cuisine
I'll honor your serene
Pre-Hallowe'en
Routine.

Lew Turco

FOR ANNIE FINCH

Dear Annie,
It's simply uncanny
How every nook and cranny
Of the evening was chummy, even clanny,
Quite diverse (but without a Hindustani --
One felt like a king but not a rani).
I fear there are not many
More rhymes...or any!
Annie.

Lew Turco

RUBLIW

Dear Lew,
I guess I'll do
a rubliw or two, too.
If it's not hard for bards like you
and Sam and Dick and Dave and who knows who,
I might as well try, too. I'll rue
the day, you say? Not true:
it's fun, though new.
Thank you,
Lew.

Annie Finch

(And happy New Year, too!)

RUBLIW FOR WILLIAM BAER

Dear Bill,
This will fulfill
My vow to write — for ill
Or good — a sort of rubliw quadrille
For each of those who helped Sam Gwynn to spill
A flagon or two of great goodwill
At my retirement squill.
Alas! there's still
No refill.

Lew Turco

RUBLIW FOR H. R. COURSEN, JR.

Dear Herb,
It was superb!
I was a bit acerb
When it was my turn to perturb
The audience. I did not try to curb
My tongue. But did I thus disturb
My students with suburb-
an noun or verb?
Absurd!

Lew Turco

RUBLIW FOR A TEACHER

Dear Lew,
Is it really true?
Am I blue? Boo hoo!
I never had a clue or cue
You flew the coop. Who's in charge of the zoo?
A gnu? A ewe? A kangaroo?
A shrew? Winnie the Pooh?
Thanks for being you.
I grew.

John Grau

RUBLIW ACCOMPANYING A
MANUSCRIPT OF SONNETS

Dear Lew,
Loved the rubliw!
Tried hard to write a few,
But instead, thought I'd just redo
Some of that old stuff — a sonnet or two,
The hearty rhymes a bit off hue,
Eternal sonic stew,
Now yours to view.
Stay coo[l]!

Stephen Murabito

RUBLIW FOR LOO-LEW

Dear Lew,
this form's translu-
cent sonic joy's a loo-
p of repetition: the rubliw,
well-named. I read your first one in my loo
this afternoon! A poem in lieu
of the sports page. Rubliw
's a true, new lu-
lu, Lew!

With friendship and shame, Dave Baker / evad rekab

RUBLIW

Dear Lew,
You are the true
Heirophant of this brew,
A yeast and barley Rubliw.
Friend, this barley's not the same old doo-doo,
This wild feast no faddish voodoo
— for you took a poet's view
And made it new
In lieu.

David A. Casagrande

RUBLIW FOR LEWIS TURCO[5]

Dear Lew,
I thought a few
lines in order here to
note I've not forgotten what you
taught, or what I learned, at least, then so clue-
less, but eager. Now, finding beau-
ty in new forms, I brew
a true rubliw
for you.

Matthew J. Spireng

FOR JESSICA SHANAHAN
LIVING IN ALASKAN WOODS[4]

Dear Jess,
You can't do less
than try to retrogress
back to times before the mess
caused by mankind. But, to my distress,
I like living insectless.
Not under dire duress
would I regress,
I guess.

Lew Turco

RUBLIW FOR VERN RUTSALA[5]

Dear Vern,
How good to learn
That it is now my turn
To honor someone I discern
To be a stylist who must one day earn
A rather large and frondy fern
In Poetry's great urn.
Don't look astern —
Be stern!

Lew Turco

THE MIDDLE GENERATION

Dear Lew,
My thanks to you
For your words good and true.
They turned my mood away from blue
Toward deeper thoughts of the happy few —
You and me, a few others, too
(And not a motley crew)
Laden with rue
And overdue.

Vern Rutsala

FOR BOB CARNES, ON HIS RETIREMENT

Dear Bob,
My ears still throb
when I recall those barb-
ershopper chords you used to lob
at us to make our chorus ring and sob.
Why have we let the decades rob
us of our song and fob
off on some mob
our job?

Lew Turco

RUBLIW FOR LEW

Dear Friend —
told you I'd send
a line or two to mend
the distance. Time's footprints offend
the orderly borders of our lives, bend
us inconsolably, then lend
us something new to spend.
Is this a trend,
Dear Friend?

Dennis Morton

RUBLIW FOR HAMLET ON HIS 400th BIRTHDAY

Dear Ham,
I guess I am
just about as damn
full of you as any clam
is full of stuffing. I simply cannot cram
you down past my diaphragm —
not another gram.
I wish you'd scram,
you ham!

Lewis Turco

RUBLIW FOR GAIL WHITE

Dear Gail,
I grew quite pale
when I found in the mail
a copy of your chapbook. "A 'stale
creampuff' once more, no doubt," I began to wail.
I read. Again I could inhale —
I heard the nightingale!
No need to quail
or flail!

Thanks,

Lewis Turco

RUBLIW FOR GEORGE O'CONNELL
On His Birthday, 16 October 2000

Dear George,
It would be gorg-
eous to do as the Borg-
ias did and take a meal to gorge
us all on your birthday. It will forge
a closer bond among us four
"jest folks." Who could want more,
George? Be food's scourge —
engorge!

Lewis Turco

RUBLIW FOR KAY PALMER
on the passing of Erwin,[6] her husband, 17 October 2000.

Dear Kay,
It's hard to say
that Erwin is gone today.
I'm sure that nothing can allay
the grief you feel, but no one can gainsay
he led a useful life. Dismay
must yield to pride. The clay
goes on its way —
we stay.

Lewis Turco

RUBLIW FOR MARGARET GROUT
On Her 100th Birthday.

Dear Mar-
garet, you are
without doubt, by far
a century's most shining star.
independent of the calendar,
here is a ringing reservoir
of lovesong poured afar
from an Alcazar
guitar.

Lew & Jean Turco

RUBLIW FOR MARTHA AND STEVEN SWERDFEGER

Scottsdale, Arizona, 18 December, 2002: "Margaret died late yesterday afternoon. Her health began to deteriorate about three weeks before her 100th birthday. She had hoped to move on even sooner."

Dear Steve
and Martha, we grieve
with you, but the sleave
of care is raveled now. Believe
the hands of time no longer can unweave
what once they wove, cannot bereave
you again, so heave
one sigh, cleave
and leave.

Lew & Jean

---

[1]This poem, together with Richard Wilbur's "For Lewis Turco," was published originally as "The Birth of a Verse Form" in *The Formalist*, viii:1, 1997 (c) William Baer, 1997; reprinted in *The Book of Forms: A Handbook of Poetics*, Third Edition, Hanover: University Press of New England, (c) Lewis Turco, 2000.
[2]Published in *The Formalist*, viii:2, 1997 (c) William Baer, 1997.
[4]Published in *The Formalist*, xlv:1, 2003 (c) William Baer, 2003.
[5]Published in *Calapooya Collage 19*, (c) Tom Ferté, 1997.
[6]Dr. Erwin Palmer was the chair of the Oswego English department who hired Lewis Turco in 1965.

FOREWORD TO *FIRST POEMS*
Donald Justice

These are the poems Lew Turco wrote in his early twenties, while he was trying out his talent, seeing which way it wanted to go, and one of the interests they are likely to have for the future is that of a literary record, the record of a poet's initiation into the rites of the craft. There is a good deal here of what some people call versifying, meaning something unpleasant, perhaps. It is as if the poet had come across a handbook on versification and set himself to working out the problems there, as the student of mathematics might do, a process sure to appall the tender-minded. The models to be found in such handbooks are, to be sure, appalling enough, clever at best and very soft. But Mr. Turco is not soft and he is very clever. One is reminded less of the H. C. Bunners of this world than of someone like Hardy, that great versifier who was also, at times, a great poet. There is something of Hardy's approach to poetry here, not that of the gloomy philosopher, but of the poet who set himself repeatedly the most trying technical problems and in solving them took and gave pleasure both.

For part of Lewis Turco's exuberance, which is everywhere in evidence, is a matter of technique. No reader can avoid noticing the variety of forms here. There are Sapphics, several of the French forms, sonnets, syllabics, and a number of what this young poet, who originated the form, calls "triversens," or triple-verse-sentences; curiously, no villanelles, no sestinas, fashionable forms at the moment. The result of all this is, on occasion, a highly agreeable kind of showing off, not far from the young Rimbaud's when he chose to make a refrain out of that impossible line, *Ithyphalliques et pioupiesques.*

A bright and productive future is the easiest thing in the world to predict for Lew Turco, who is just turning twenty-six. Meanwhile, reading this book is a little like listening to a gifted musician practicing scales, arpeggios, and the sonatas of Clementi. Very pleasant to hear, of course, and I think most of us will want to take tickets for the concert.

A POETICS OF THE PSYCHE
by Mary Doll

THOSE FAMILIAR WITH LEWIS TURCO'S WRITING agree that it presents a world both like and not like our own. Its fascination lies in its ambiguity, true to the promptings of inner life. Ray Bradbury has said, "Everything he writes about in *The Inhabitant* is part of my own real or remembered world." The poet Philip Booth has commented, "The Ferry" [from *American Still Lifes*] crosses me over to wherever it is that all true poems tug and pull." And the American literary critic Hyatt. H. Waggoner has compared Turco's worlds to Emerson's "forms," saying that "he is really, it seems to me, doing what Emerson meant by 'sharing the circuit of things through forms,' making the forms...translucid so the light can shine through."

Critics of Turco's earlier work, however, focused less on its presentation of psychological truths than on its preoccupation with technique. For some, Turco's experiments with language and form got in the way of the poem itself, making the work seem marked by "easy virtuosity." For others, Turco's world was too static. As Henry Carlile put it, "Turco has a fondness for negative declarations which tend almost to negate themselves in the process...one might ask: if nothing is happening, why write about it?"

These criticisms stem, in part, from Turco's interest in language as substance, to be molded so as to produce layers of sensory impressions. With a keen ear for language and a delight in old words, he was in many instances producing poems that were, as William Heyen said, "too stiff, metrically, or too pretty, or too ingenious, or too heavily moral and wise." Perhaps in response to these comments, Lewis Turco created an alter ego, "Wesli Court," an anagram of his own name. As a traditional versifier, Court could publish as many metrically "correct," formalistically clever works as Turco desired. One book of poems, *Courses in Lambents* (1977); two poetry chapbooks, *Curses and Laments* (1978), and *The Airs of Wales* (1981); and one children's story, *Murgatroyd and Mabel* (1978) have been published to Wesli Court's credit.

But the other area of concern to critics — Turco's still worlds — relates to his new and different sensibility. This is a sensibility that reveals not human subjects and ego consciousness so much as a live quality in objects and nature. In his best work, Turco shows what it is to 'see through a glass, darkly' "from the other side." The critic who is firmly planted in Aristotelian poetics will have difficulty adjusting to this non-mimetic, nonexpressive universe. And yet, as Bradbury, Booth, and Waggoner among others have noted, this "other" world brings us closer to our own psychic depths in a way akin to Emerson or to the Zen poet. In defining the Zen poet in his college text *Poetry: An Introduction Through Writing* (1973) Turco could well be offering a definition of his own poetic voice. The Zen poet, he writes, "is attempting to put himself into the place of the thing perceived — he is empathizing with the object; more, he is trying to become one with the object."

I

First Poems (1960), a selection of the Book Club for Poetry, contains pieces that were written during Turco's navy and undergraduate years and reveals his musical ear for language. As Donald Justice, in his foreword, comments: "reading this book is a little like listening to a gifted musician practicing scales, arpeggios, and the sonatas of Clementi."

Divided into three sections with a total of thirty-eight poems, the book shows a range of technique and imagination that marks the later work as well. "Dirge à la Dylan" is a clear illustration of Turco's fondness for the sound of words. His ear for Dylan Thomas's sensual playfulness can be heard in the opening stanza: "When I was a curled boy, short and long- / shadowed beneath an apple moon, / I peeled my dreams out of cider skies / and toasted them crisp each fiery noon."

A less derivative poem is "Chant of Seasons," which allows the singing voice to emerge with sadness. The stanza on the season of fall is remarkable for its compactness of sound and theme:

CHANT OF SEASONS

What may one do when springtime's come —
    When springtime's come,
But welcome it unquestioning
As every bride accepts her ring?
    Ask any groom: the future's dumb;
    The present is the vocal thing
    When springtime's come.

What can one know when summer's here —
    When summer's here,
Beside the fact that sun is sun
And that the world is overrun
    By surging life: no thin veneer,
    But deep? Too deep to be undone
    When summer's here.

What of the time when fall's returned —
    When fall's returned?
Then listen to the wind and leaves
During the night: the day deceives.
    Beyond the frosts there is discerned
    The womb within which death conceives,
    When fall's returned.

What's to be done when winter's loose —
When winter's loose?
Sense then the sharpened stars and know
The bold immensity of snow;
    Grant bone a glimpse of the abstruse
    Finis that it must undergo...,
      When winter's loose.

Here is Turco's most meditated-upon season, fall, with all of its ampli-
fied meanings. The theme of cyclical time as opposed to linear time sets
up a Romantic dichotomy between nature and man, eternity and
mortality. Embedded in "Fall" is also the Judeo-Christian idea of
Adam's fall through Eve: of the burden man must bear because of
woman's womb "within which death conceives." Even in this early
chant of the seasons, Turco shows signs of attempting to breach the gap
of traditional oppositions posed by a Romantic imagination. By going
beyond fall to winter, with its "bold immensity of snow," he allows his
poetic imagination to play with cold, to "grant bone a glimpse of the
abstruse / Finis that it must undergo...."

Aside from its pivotal effect on human time, fall also connotes to
Turco the pivot point between intellect and imagination, as in the
beginning of academic life each fall semester. In "Poems for an Old
Professor," a series of four poems which Richard Eberhart said showed
Turco's profundity [see bibliography, below], the poet again sets up
categorical oppositions. Here, the old, dry life of an academic professor
who teaches Milton is juxtaposed against the imagined chance for a new
life offered from Milton's text by Eve.

The old professor represents routine: all that which can be delegated
to keeping meaning clear, explicated within the bounds of written texts.
But Eve represents ritual. Her "deplorable behavior" is the text of lived
experience — the poetry of life that lies between the lines. The
professor, in his quest for clarity, is in a sense deconstructed by the very

text he manipulates. What is, in the classroom and for the professor, an academic search for intellectual meaning becomes, in the poem, an opportunity to search for the lost paradise of male consciousness.

One theme in *First Poems* has been consistent throughout all of Turco's work, the theme of seeing. Mirrors, glass, pools, water, eyes are frequent images; and the myth of Narcissus, with its motif of seeing the reflected self, is a recurring myth. Talking about his own convictions in what could be a gloss of this theme, Turco said in a recent interview with Donald Masterson [see bibliography, below]: "I believe it is only possible for a person to define himself in terms of others, as one sees oneself reflected in the eyes and actions of others. I believe that one sees oneself most clearly mirrored in the people and things that surround one."

"Street Meeting" from *First Poems* exemplifies this credo perfectly. Two people meet after years of separation. While their words are platitudes, their eyes are pools for self-understanding:

STREET MEETING

I saw him on the street.
    His flesh was heavy.
For years we had not met:
    Time takes its levy,
Returning ounce for hour.
        But the eyes I'd known
Had stayed the same though flesh constricted bone.

His eyes owned all the past —
    I saw it staring,
Bewildered, not at rest,
    Still full of daring,
But fettered now by the hoar
        Of revolving clocks:
A hurt, unlikely witch within its stocks.

I watched the troubled look
His face reflected
And knew he'd pick my lock
Had time defected.
But each of us could hear
Wary sentries call
And answer in the long, resounding hall.

We spoke in platitudes,
Each of us helpless,
The victims of our moods
And of our losses:
The present was the heir
Of our common past.
The future would inherit all at last.

We parted. Each of us
Had fanned an ember.
We'd shared another loss
And would remember.
But time was still for hire:
He walked off alone.
When next we meet our prisons will have grown.

By seeing loneliness and loss in another's eyes, the narrator transcends ego consciousness to glimpse something of the existential depths of the human psyche.

In what remains the most perceptive critical comment to date of Turco's work, Stanley Romaine Hopper — [in the *Introduction to Riverside Poetry 3*, edited by Marianne Moore, Howard Nemerov, and Alan Swallow (1958), see bibliography, below] — praised "Street Meeting" for the release of what he called "poetical meaning." He said that "subordinating the persons to the deeper meaning of events, and by fusing the contradictory elements in the language...the 'poetical' meaning of the encounter is made to emerge." Hopper recognized early on in Turco's work what has become perhaps its unique poetic quality: the elevation of psychological over personal truths.

II

In *Awaken, Bells Falling*, Turco's [third] collection, a trend toward an ever-deepening psychological vision is evident. John Ciardi praised Turco's "gift of seeing things"; Richard Eberhart commented on his "shrewd eye on the world"; and Mary Oliver [see bibliography, below] had this to say: "In building his poems Mr. Turco has a gift for the exciting image — a way of combining objects from different existences that helps us to see sharply and freshly."

These observations about seeing and objects suggest that by the late 1960s Turco had found the theme and images necessary for the poetic voice he was developing. Some poems, however, still evidenced an infatuation with verbal dance, as in "The Forest of My Seasons." A sestina, with six end-words of the first stanza repeated in particular order for the next five stanzas, it uses as basic building blocks important Turco words: snow, wind, horns, woods, can, and shade. But because sonics and puns are allowed to overtake meaning, the poem seems more the work of Wesli Court mocking poetistic formalistic tradition.

Not so "The Old Professor and the Sphinx." Here Turco's paradoxical imagination is felt. He ponders again the dilemma of the professor who has a poet's soul ("a phoenix nesting in my skull") whose work with words seems lifeless. This he contrasts with a forgotten power within language, known by our ancestors, by Oriental art, and by poetry: "I know the poems on my shelves speak with / one another in an / ancient language I have somehow forgotten." For a poet-professor caught in the desert of academe, the challenge is to unlock language's hidden magic. Turco's extended metaphor of Egypt illuminates the richness of the idea of silent speakings:

THE OLD PROFESSOR AND THE SPHINX

It is a dry word in a dry book
drying out my ear. I squat and swallow
   my tongue here in this chair,
the desert of my desk, summer bare, spreading
like a brown horizon into regions grown arid
with erudition. A caravan of books treks

   stolidly across my eyes while I,
   the Sphinx, a phoenix nesting in my skull,
      pry into inkwells and
   gluepots seeking the universal solvent.
There is none. The pages as I turn them sound like sand
rattling in the sec temples of a beast gone to

   earth with the sun. I lie caught in my
   creaking dune, shifting with the wind of the
      pharaohs, wondering if,
   somewhere, I have not missed my valley. Upon
the walls of my office there are Oriental prints
hanging stiff as papyrus, whispering their brown

   images into the silent air.
   I know the poems on my shelves speak with
      one another in an
   ancient language I have somehow forgotten.
If there is rainfall, I recall, the desert blossoms —
but I have somewhere lost the natural prayer

   and instinctual rites of the blood
   which can conjure clouds in seasons of drought.
      There is but ritual

remaining; no honey is in the lion's
hide; my temples have mumbled to ruin: they endure
disuse and despair. An archaeologist of

cabinets and drawers, I exhume
paperclip skeletons, the artifacts
of millennia: red
ball-point pens with nothing in their veins, pencils
like broken lances, and notebook citadels empty
of citizens — the crusader has squandered his

talents on bawds, grown hoary in their
service. The town is sacked: the bawds are gone
to tame younger legions.
Look into my sarcophagus: the tapes are
sunken over my hollow sockets. Slowly the waste
swallows my oasis like a froth of spittle.

"The Old Professor and the Sphinx" marks a turning point in
Turco's development as a poet. By moving away from traditional form
toward a concentrated use of touchstone words, Turco permits the
words themselves to release what Hopper referred to as "poetic
meaning," fusing sound, form, and idea. In the juxtaposition of
professor and sphinx, Turco is really suggesting that his function as a
poet is like that of the archaeologist, digging down beneath surfaces,
exhuming meaning from hidden depths. In such a way, the professor
discovers what the poet knows: the hermetic roots of language.

Integral to such a shift toward word-conjuring is the development
of voice. Increasingly, what speaks in a Turco poem is a consciousness
of objects and nature. *Awaken, Bells Falling* is a hauntingly distanced
work where the It rather than the I is evoked. As William Heyen
remarked [see bibliography, below], "The sensibility behind these
poems is willing to allow its subjects to Be rather than constantly
Become." "School Drawing" and "Mice in the Sunday Walls" are two

fine examples. In the former, the poet meditates on his daughter's crayoned drawing. He sees a surrealistic world containing only a road, a windmill, and a crayoned sun. There is no connection among the objects; they just are. But by using his poet's imagination to see through images, to find meaning only in images, he allows the power of imagistic statement to emerge: "It is burning / and there is no wind."

"Mice in the Sunday Walls" also focuses on the nonhuman world:

MICE IN THE SUNDAY WALLS

The gray rain, like mice scurrying about the house,
nibbles the edges of a moldy afternoon.
    Sunday's trap is set for us to trigger.
    The doorbell. The door. The whole hall hungry,
its yellow stairs snapping at our laces; the old
    lady mewing in the parlor, arching
her aching back - O! The same old tom in the same

armchair rising, dragging his sagging tail
over the carpet to welcome us back.
    The cool cat gone, off in his Olds down the alley,
    the motor purring convertibly; seduction
sloshing contentiously in the gas tank:
    gone, man, gone. Sunday rustles in the walls. We four
sit lapping the skim of our duty call.

This is the way the old folks seem at last. Death sprawls
on the couch to doze an age. But metaphor will
    not suffice to crystallize aversion;
    nor simile, our compassion. There is
nowhere to go, nothing to see, little to do
    here in childhood's hall of mirrors. Backward
and forward, reflected in each-other's vision,

distorted images of our common
love separate, then merge, then fade and fail.
We talk. Quietly at first, for fear of shadows.
Days, like mice, have overgenerated. They now
outnumber the old folks' hungers. Soon we
will leave, and no one will reflect on anyone
for very long. Nor too deeply. Nor far.

Again, a paradox of speaking-silence presents itself. The situation juxtaposes human non-communication with nonhuman speech: "Sunday's trap is set for us to trigger / The doorbell. The door. The whole hall hungry / its yellow stairs snapping at our laces." The poet's duty-call on Sunday reveals a strong sense of nothingness: "nowhere to go, nothing to see, little to do / here in childhood's hall of mirrors." And yet, as in a Frost poem, the bleakness of such blank horizons where one reflects neither "too deeply. Nor far" provokes insight. The point is that silence prompts the things of the world to present themselves to the eye of the beholder.

III

Although *The Inhabitant* was Turco's next published work, *Pocoangelini: A Fantography and Other Poems* (1971) was written first. In tone, the Poco poems represent a departure from the objective perspective discussed above. Through the guise of a madcap trickster figure named Pocoangelini, these poems show Turco's earlier Romantic themes from an upside-down point of view. Such serious ideas as death, time, darkness, and silence are turned into comic songs. Poco allows Turco to imagine his dark themes differently.

One manifestation of this difference is the arrangement of poems into series. Forty-two separate poems, with a prologue and epilogue, constitute the work, suggesting that the voice of Poco is not unilateral, but various, and that truth has many voices. The effect this has on the

53

reader's understanding of character is profound. For what Turco shows is a non-Aristotelian character type who resists the demands of plot and linear development. As in the tradition of the fool or the trickster, Poco's character can never fully be revealed: that is his triumph over time.

Turco's delight in the imagination is evident in the Poco poems by the breadth of adventures, dialogues, and soliloquies of his character. In #28, for example, Poco assumes the voice of Pan: musical, sensual, natural: "If my song wears an old blanket / it hides young fleas. / My hoof plucks no mandolin. / Listen to this tune, hairy as a donkey." He is nature and nature is he: "spearing the grottoes between his toes" (#25). Imagination can, just as well, picture winter as Pan — "that old man with hooves" who can be seen "goring the white air," and "tearing shreds / out of the moon" (#29). To be able to imagine coldness with precision is a feat of such psychological triumph that Poco can "thrust his tongue" at it and all it connotes.

These flights of fancy give wing, as well, to the dark themes. Poco is not grounded in literal reality, like some flat-foot cop (#10) or like a Western male hero — Adam, say, or Mars, or Odysseus, or the unnamed male quester, a conglomerate of all three, who, in #21, is a victim of his own tunnel vision, unable to see deeply or to find the hidden treasures of language. This anti-hero, Poco sees, uses language as a weapon: "Glib / rolled words in his hand — a journal / held like a gun," hoping thus to kill off the monsters of darkness. But Pocoangelini, as trickster, fool, or angel, is characterized from the imagination, which can both "see" the dark and "hear" the silence, as in # 11:

> Pocoangelini's house has wings
>   lining its walls,
> dark eyes that see in the dark —
>   darts, feathering calls
>   in the pine halls;

grass and the smell of seed,
the spider's net
stretched from shadow to shade
to catch the owl's saw-whet
voice in a sunset

tangle of silk. The night
is a great falcon
circling the weathervane,
ears tuned to the unbroken
silence, the word unspoken.

With Pocoangelini, and certainly with the other series poems in that collection — *The Sketches* [originally published in 1962 as part of a chapbook titled *The Sketches of Lewis Turco and Livevil: A Mask*] and *Bordello* [published separately in its complete form as a portfolio of poem-prints with the printmaker George O'Connell in 1996] — Turco was working with voice. The various speakers are Others: "Guido the Ice-House Man," "Uncle Larry," "Miss Mary Belle" from *The Sketches*. They are "Hank Fedder" or "Lafe Grat" from *Bordello*. They are not the poet. By donning a mask of the Other, in the manner of Edwin Arlington Robinson or Edgar Lee Masters, Turco was developing the voices of America, finding in them a more general expression of the human condition than that afforded by any narrow personal idiom.

IV

The Inhabitant continues and deepens this search for voice. Here Turco finds a symbolic structure, the house, entirely consistent with what was becoming a poetics of the psyche. For Freud and Jung alike, the house is symbolic of the self with its arrangement of upper and lower floors corresponding to conscious and unconscious layers of the psyche. Turco makes use of this symbol in *The Inhabitant* in order to show that his unnamed quester inhabits a structure, himself, that is multilayered, mysterious, yet capable of transformation.

In this series of poems, the title refers to the self's search for home in a house where each room makes its appeal. As he moves through doors the Inhabitant journeys deeper into his own secret places, discovering "mathoms" — useless treasures — in the attic and monsters in the basement. He is a listener and a watcher, a stranger inside his own habitation. But because he wanders, listens, and sees, the Inhabitant is able to discover how to dwell with darkness. The seven-part concluding poem called "The Dwelling House" reworks the Genesis story with the suggestion that, through sensory awakening, man can be molded anew.

That Turco intended his vision to be psychological is clear. "Poetry is capable," he said in the Masterson interview, "of touching the deepest portions of the human psyche.... We are still after our deepest selves, and poetry...has always been capable of getting into these levels of existence, of being, and making them conscious." "The Kitchen" is one example of how life's particulars speak to the male psyche. The Inhabitant, in the kitchen with his wife and daughter, is the only one who tunes into the sounds of the dishwasher's "hum and bite." Its cycle suggests to his ears the cycle of life:

THE KITCHEN

In the kitchen the dishwasher is eating the dishes. The Inhabitant listens to the current of digestion — porcelain being ground, silver wearing thin, the hum and bite of the machine.

His wife does not hear it — she is humming, not listening. But the Inhabitant is aware of movement in the cupboards, of the veriest motion — the cast-iron skillet undergoing metamorphosis, perhaps, becoming its name: the wives' spider spinning beneath the counter, weaving and managing, waiting for the doors to open.

Each cup has its voice, each saucer its ear, and the thin chant planes between the shelves, touching the timbres of glass and crystal as it passes. The gentleman listens, is touched to the bone by this plainsong — he feels his response in the marrow's keening.

But the women do not — neither the elder nor the child — sense the music their things make. Their lips move, a column of air rises like steam, and there is something in a minor key sliding along the wall, touching the face of a plastic clock, disturbing the linen calendar beside the condiments.

It is as though, the Inhabitant reflects, the women are spinning. It is as though, while he waits, they weave bindings among the rooms; as though the strands of tune were elements of a sisterhood of dishes, the ladies, the spider in the cabinet, even of the dishwasher, done now with its grinding, which contributes a new sound — a continuo of satiety — to the gray motet the kitchen is singing.

For Turco men — not women — feel their mortality: in the ear, in the bone. Their senses are "keener," but as in the pun, this only makes them mourn their fate. Women, progenitors of the human cycle, are oblivious to sound's sense. And fate is literally in the hands of women who, like their mythic counterparts, are spinners and weavers of the threads of life, in whose web the human condition is caught. The poem's circular ending fuses form with theme in a subtly interesting way. The poet shows that even the closed cycle of life can have its musical dance.

Other poems in the series bring out the psychomythic undertone of the Inhabitant's searchings, making them, as Conrad Aiken remarked, a poetry of "whole meaning." The Inhabitant's descent down the basement stairs to retrieve his daughter's doll becomes a descent into "silence spinning." In his search for lost treasure the Inhabitant is like Orpheus, whose visit to retrieve Eurydice from Hades reveals myth's fear of sight's power. "Turning to look" is prohibited. The Inhabitant's mission is fraught with this dread importance:

THE BASEMENT

The Inhabitant descends to find the child's lost doll. The door, the narrow stair, the snaky mop on sentry at the stairhead — these have been managed.

The light here is yellow; the walls drink its treacle, turn it to cobwebbing and dust, a faint odor of coal left over from another year.

The walls drink sound as well — the Inhabitant's thin whistle, the squeal of the furnace flywheel turning, saying small things, informing the spider's fretwork of minuscule agonies. The voice of a mouse is strapped to silence spinning.

Beside the set-tubs the toys lie in their boxes. In the sinks, stagnant water ebbs and tides; the curved hose of the washer arches downward, but never touches the surface — never quite touches the gray surface rising and falling in the clogged pipes, the storm drains under the cellar leading outward and downward.

The Inhabitant will find her, must find her for the yearning child. She will be in the boxes, clothed in rags, wearing her painted smile and a scraped eye, its metal beginning to corrode.

His fingers brush through the castoff things: some blocks, a partial deck of minicards — King of Spades and Queen of Hearts, Pinocchio without his rubber nose. The toys drift in the dusk like the buoys of time, shadowmarks on darkness.

Upstairs the child is waiting, having remembered, wanting the past as palpable as chain. But this is carrying water in a sieve: a toy boat rides with a ragged sail, adrift, its anchor dragging through the dust like stars.

Here she lies at last, the lost toy in her apron, smiling like yarn out of the yawning box. Take her and carry her to the stair as the wheel stands still, the tides lie quiet in the soapy tubs; do not glance back nor at the ragged doll or she shall be left at the stairhead beneath the writhing mop, and the wheel will begin to spin, its voice to whine; the webs will net dust in the billowing corners when the light goes out.

The treasures one puts one's eyes on are both life-sustaining and life-threatening, equally.

Turco's concentration in "The Looking-Glass" is also on the eye as window to the soul. Invoking Narcissus and the phoenix, he provides an arresting image of eye preening in its vision. The image suggests an insight into the Narcissus myth: that to fall in love with one's reflected vision is not the same thing as to fall in love with one's face; rather, one loves image. To preen thus is to be transported to another place of being and so, transformed:

THE LOOKING-GLASS

Once in a while
    the eye

circles like a hawk
    comes down

in a place never
    inhabited by

anything animate anything sharp
    or whole

and there lying in
    its circle

of smooth things the
    eye preens

in its own vision
    before it

rakes the wind again
    and rises

into the sun the
    fierce air.

The mythic spiritualism of *The Inhabitant*, which Conrad Aiken described enthusiastically as "the best new poem I've read in something like thirty years," is carried even deeper in *American Still Lifes* (1981). What emerges is an increasingly translucent vision, where the eye is in all things. As William Heyen noted, Turco was moving his poetry into "the still-point." Hyatt H. Waggoner [for both references, see bibliography, below], in commenting on Emerson's notion of the true poet, implied that Turco's insights were guided by a true poet's sense of imagination, which "does not come by study, but by the intellect being where and what it sees."

V

Waggoner's remarks were made in reference to the poems that appeared in a chapbook, *The Weed Garden* (1973). Both it and another chapbook, *Seasons of the Blood* (1980), can be considered preparing ground for *American Still Lifes*. In *Seasons*, particularly, the poet's use of Japanese forms — the mondo, katauta, sedoka, haiku, and senryu among others — encouraged a dialectical Western mind to ponder the virtues of Eastern paradox. The Japanese basic unit of three lines was the perfect vehicle for Turco, who was building his poetry more and more around imagery and sensory impression.

VI

American Still Lifes contains three sections: "Twelve Moons," "Still Lifes," and "Autumn's Tales." Together they provide a kind of Eastern response to the West's problem with time as history or mortality. In their celebration of imagination's eternity, the poems represent an artistic and personal triumph for Turco, whose struggle with the theme of death finds reconciliation here in a timelessness of the senses trained to listen to stillness. All of nature becomes Turco's reflecting pool: darkness "sings" and silence "is hanging fire behind the moon." Nature's world creates strong sensory impressions in flame, wind, and the whickering of horses. Against these particulars human life is stilled, made to become but a part of larger cyclical patterns.

"Twelve Moons," for example, sets a tone of biding or waiting. The theme retells the idea of the Fall of Man; but Turco, in playing with the theme, opens the idea out to reveal its rich substructures. Fall is lived, experienced, sensed, not just understood as a doctrine of sin and redemption. Almost every poem, indeed, employs the word fall. Light falls, shadows fall, fish and seagulls fall; a chestnut falls. There is snowfall and footfall. Evening falls. Such concentration invites us to bide time with a basic Judeo-Christian motif, so as to hear in its soundings a newness.

"Still Lifes" and "Autumn's Tales" also play with our senses. In both, Turco uses language to reawaken our eyes so that we may see in a still life canvas or in the frame of a camera many other images. The poems resonate so deeply because Turco's trope, fall, is explored with completeness and yet restraint. By turning doctrine into poetry, Turco shows that language is, at root, metaphor: capable of carrying us over into new awarenesses.

"Still Lifes," a series of twenty-nine poems, presents a history of the New World from Colonial to modern times. Without explicit time connections, history becomes poeticized. Time is really memory, a deeper collective history of the human race. Images inhabit such structures from our past as a tollhouse, a covered bridge, and a trestle. That these old structures are visited by ghosts or by an unnamed consciousness of the poem suggests a psychological truth Turco had been developing since *The Inhabitant*. Old forms are containers for living images. Their appeal lies in what Suzanne Langer calls "semblance," or "likeness": they are truths of a different order. As Langer puts it, "The function of 'semblance' is to give forms a new embodiment in purely qualitative, unreal instances, setting them free from their normal embodiment in real things so that they may be recognized in their own right...." Turco's achievement is in bringing an Eastern prosody of the senses to bear on the familiar themes and things of Western culture. In so doing he petitions us to let go of our traditional responses.

The final poem of "Autumn's Tales," "The Vista," is an example of Turco's fusion of form, idea, image, and sound to create "semblance." The other eight poems in the series are about fall; they capture, as in a camera's frozen moment, the coming of a storm. In the last poem nature is trapped by a blizzard; but although the sense of being devoured by snow is strong, Turco maintains a tone of calm detachment. The descent into the earth's maw is simply seasonal:

THE VISTA

As the storm comes now like a cage of dark air,
the snowflakes fall before it:
they have been frightened by nothing
into their descent.

The trees are filled with small cries.
The avenue becomes a river of still forms.

The cars are trapped in frost fire;
the eye of a pond witnesses what it can
before the cataract steals its sight.
Houses settle into their yards,
farms into their fields and fences.
The hills rise over the valley,
and the river is lost.

Yeats once said that poetry is what a man writes out of his quarrel with himself. Throughout his poetic career Turco has dared venture into his own fears and silences, into the idea of death, and into America's lost past. In *First Poems* a Romantic imagination was seeking ways to overcome the splits between mortality and eternity, mind and spirit, literalism and metaphor, comedy and tragedy. Exploring the traditional forms and genres of Western poetry — everything from narratives and satires to accentual-syllabics and sestinas — he demonstrated his command over language. His Wesli Court poems were part of that demonstration. But he never forgot the advice of his first critic to drop the confessional I. Out of this quarrel he found other voices from which his themes were distilled. In the forms of Eastern culture Turco's poetry reached a new level: not his command, but language's depths were plumbed, and archetypes surfaced.

From the beginning Turco's themes have remained consistent: darkness, winter, silence, fall. Writing with the cold eye of the Zen poet, he has provided a stunning response to Western pessimism, as seen in the tradition of the Fall; and Western egoism, as seen in traditional interpretations of Narcissism. His poetry uncovers grace in the void and the images with which to see that grace. His words petition modern Western consciousness to look more deeply into the dimension of depth. And if Turco's world is fantastical and still, this is because of his reverence for imagination, without which our world is not fleshed. Through him we come to see what lies just behind all things, even if the vista is but a blanket of white snow.

MAKING THE LANGUAGE DANCE AND GO DEEP
by Donald Masterson, edited by Jack Welch

THIS INTERVIEW WAS CONDUCTED BY DONALD MASTERSON in the fall of 1980. At the time, the State University of New York College at Oswego, where Lewis Turco is Professor of English and Director of the Program in Writing Arts, was hosting the third S.U.N.Y. state-wide writers' festival. Turco's chapbook, *Seasons of the Blood*, had just appeared, and he was putting the finishing touches on his *American Still Lifes*, which would be published in September, 1981. Masterson and Turco met in the poet's campus office and discussed at great length (easily two and a half times the length seen here) the history, the teaching, and the craft of poetry, along with the requisite attitude of the professional poet.

Masterson. would you define the difference, if there is one, between one who writes poems occasionally, and publishes them, and someone who can be certifiably listed as a poet?

Turco. I imagine that what you're talking about is the difference between the professional and the amateur poet. Some people will no doubt feel that the phrase "professional poet" is a pejorative expression, but it seems to me that one is a professional poet when one dedicates one's life to writing poetry. I think that's the sole criterion one can apply. If poetry is an avocation, or if it's merely a means to an end — that is, let's say, a means to getting a job teaching, or of putting forward a political point of view — then I don't feel one can call oneself a professional poet. But that would be my criterion for almost anything; anyone who dedicates his or her life to a particular vocation is, in my estimation, a professional.

Masterson. What are the manifestations of a dedication to writing poetry?

Turco. I don't suppose that's a question that can be answered by anyone except oneself. Other people are going to have to examine one's academic and publishing record when someone who calls himself a "poet" applies for a teaching position or something similar, but I doubt that anyone but the writer himself can judge the depth of his own commitment.

Masterson. You wouldn't necessarily say that a person be considered a professional poet because he or she has two or three books or work in a number of periodicals? That would not meet the criterion?

Turco. Absolutely not. But if the dedication is to language, to its specific gravity, its meanings and associations, to its dance — its sounds, imagery, even to the way it looks on the page — then the person in question might call himself or herself a poet. There are many fine writers who were unpublished in their lifetimes who were obviously professional poets — Emily Dickinson, for instance, and Gerard Manley Hopkins; and there are some who have published a great deal who were obviously amateurs, as for instance Walt Whitman, who was much more interested in his "message" than in the language that carried the message. Emily Dickinson was the professional writer, for her life was totally dedicated to writing poetry, and Whitman was the amateur because his life was dedicated, not to writing poetry, but to propagandizing for a "new, American" kind of poetry and for various liberal causes and attitudes. Whitman was sometimes what I call an "agonist" — one who agonizes over and about what poetry is or ought to be, or who writes poems about poetry.

Masterson. But wouldn't some say that this is in a way very appropriate for Whitman because he stands at the beginning of modern poetry, and the agonizing would all have been very necessary at that particular moment in American literary history?

Turco. That's all perfectly true, but "agonist" is merely one of three categories we've been discussing — "professional, amateur, and agonist." The agonist is neither a professional nor an amateur, when you come right down to it; he or she is a public relations person for poetry, or a theorizer for poetry. But actually, Whitman was not so much the main theorist of what would after him be called "modernist" poetry; rather, Emerson was. Emerson was almost a pure agonist. Whitman merely put into practice the agonies of Emerson. In his poems, I think, Whitman was not so much interested in the dance of language as in, for one thing, the propagation of his own ego, and for another, in propagandizing for a liberal America.

Masterson. If that's the case for Whitman, then in some ways his inheritor in the 20th century was William Carlos Williams who was also in his own way a propagandist and one who made great claims for a liberal America in his poetry, but I gather that you would not claim that he was an agonist, but a true professional.

Turco. Whether I'm being clear or not, you seem to be getting what I mean by these terms. Yes, Williams was a professional. It wasn't in his poetry that he did all the agonizing you point to; it was in his letters to young poets and in what little prose he wrote, sometimes in his long poem *Paterson* and in *In the American Grain*. He was, in most of his poems, very much interested in the dance of language. He maintained that he wasn't interested so much in sound, but in image — he was one of the prime members of the school of poets called "Imagists" — but in fact he was also interested in the sonic dance of language. He invented a prosody which would do rhythmically for him what he wanted the language to do. He talked about the "breath pause," by which he meant grammatics: each line was to be a breath-length phrase. This was the same sort of idea as the five- or seven-syllable line of Japanese poetry, these lengths being just right to give vent to an "utterance," an emotive, short phrase, often a question or an answer, which is at the prosodic base of all the Japanese forms from the katauta to the haiku.

Masterson. You have worked with the Williams line, I believe, and with the eighteen-line form he invented, which you call the "triversen" in *The Book of Forms* [1968].

Turco. Yes. In fact the first dozen poems, called "Twelve Moons," forthcoming in my *American Still Lifes*, are all written in the Williams triversen form or in the triversen stanza. One is called

SEED MOON

In the night there was a crescent
    thin as a breath
        floating in the sky.

Now the sun has quickened;
    it sprays the green meadows
        with drops of light.

Birds pierce the trees
    along the lake where grass
        thrusts through the bluff.

In the houses of the village
    there is the scent of savors —
        the women move and the men rise.

Soon the earth will fill with voices,
    the sounds of loam turning;
        the sun will stretch to fill the sky,

and in the woodland the deer
will sample the air,
    lift their heads to listen.

Masterson. Likewise, you've worked with the Japanese forms, I assume?

Turco. All the poems in my *Seasons of the Blood* are in the Japanese forms. This one is a sedoka:

DIALOGUE

I am wearing blue
in honor of the sky. Shall
you wear green to honor earth?

I will don rainbows:
I will wear snow on my back —
white, allcolor forever.

Masterson. I hear the similarity in phrasing, but the tone is quite different.

Turco. Of course. The two books attempt different things. *American Still Lifes* has an American feel, and *Seasons of the Blood* has an Oriental one...I hope.

Masterson. The point you make, therefore, is that, even though Williams was a proselytizer for a certain kind of poetry, in a way a kind of American prophet following Whitman, his proselytizing was done outside of the realm of his poetry for the most part?

Turco. Now you've really put your finger on what a certain kind of American "poetry" is all about. It isn't about language, it isn't about art, it's about...patriotism, I suppose I'd have to say. There are two main traditions in poetry. There's what I call "priest poetry," which is derived specifically from the liturgies and practices of various religions — prayers, incantations, sermons, and so forth; the tradition is millennia old. Others would call it Platonic poetry, I suppose, or Dionysian poetry. It is the romantic tradition. Then there's the so-called "art" poetry which is derived from work songs — rhythmic songs that women have always sung to their children while they were churning butter or whatever — which has nothing to do with religion. This is social poetry, Apollonian or Aristotelian, the classical tradition. American poetry, when it was defined by Emerson and Whitman, was defined specifically as priest poetry, but a particular kind, in order to distinguish it from European priest poetry. American poetry was to be anti-formal poetry, intuitive, "organic."

Whitman, as the prime priest poet of America, was concerned with mythologizing American experience in this "new" way. But Dickinson, who was interested not at all in vision or prophecy or anything like that (though she was most certainly interested in religious questions), was contemporaneously writing excellent art poetry which was also quintessentially and unmistakably American. It seems to me that priest poetry tends to be amateur and that art poetry tends to be professional.

Masterson. You see Whitman, then, as a kind of chauvinist?

Turco. Certainly. As a matter of fact, it seems to me that Whitman did something that was very clever indeed along that line. When he first began to write in the pages of *The Brooklyn Eagle* he was writing rhyming, metering verse, and anyone who wants to look up this stuff will find that it's terrible. Completely incompetent. The best surviving example of this sort of Whitman doggerel is "O, Captain, My Captain!" In verse Whitman had a tin ear. He could not handle traditional techniques. But then he discovered the Biblical systems of parallel prose writing, and he equated himself with America. Ever since, we have been idolizing him — I mean that literally. We have idolized a bad writer but a great chauvinist.

Masterson. How do you explain, then, William Carlos Williams' dedication to Whitman's work?

Turco. That is a myth. Some people claim that Williams is in "the Whitman tradition," but Hyatt H. Waggoner, in his book *American Poets from the Puritans to the Present* [1968; revised edition, 1984] claims that Williams knew very little about Whitman, and Waggoner is a pro-Whitman scholar. Williams was interested in only part of what Whitman was interested in. Waggoner talks about the mainstream of American poetry deriving from Whitman and Emerson, but then he makes distinctions among those poets who derive directly from Emerson's Transcendentalist credo, those who derive directly from Whitman's prose-poetry practice, and those who derive from a combination of the two. William Carlos Williams derives, I would think, primarily from Whitman's practice, not from Emerson's agonism. That is to say, Williams was interested in Whitman's attempt to write in prose, thus getting away from traditional British practice. But rather than write prose poems, Williams invented a verse prosody — variable accentuals — that looks, acts, and sounds like prose most of the time. In this way he was like Whitman superficially.

Williams was also interested in the "common man," as Whitman professed to be, but in Williams' poetry the reader will find real people. In Whitman's poetry we find laborers mentioned and over-mentioned in catalogs of people, but the only person one will find is Whitman himself, or at least an image of himself that he projected. Williams was interested in Everyman; Whitman was interested in himself as the symbol of Everyman.

Those poets who derive primarily from Emerson might be people like Denise Levertov, people who are not so much interested in the way language works as they are in various kinds of propaganda. Levertov, of course, became the prototypical poet of the Vietnam War protest. Her major reputation rests on her anti-war poetry.

Masterson. What direction or directions has your poetry taken in the past few years? Judging from *Seasons of the Blood* [1980] and *American Still Lifes* [1981], you still write eclectically. I'd also be interested in a long-term picture of where it's been and where it's going.

Turco. When I began to write I was still a child, and I had a simple objective in mind. I enjoyed reading, and I felt that if I could, when I became an adult I would like to be able to do for other people what writers had done for me. I wanted to create worlds that were more interesting, perhaps, than the world I inhabited at the moment; to create characters who were interesting, and who would give insight into lives I could not lead myself, into human nature as it embodied itself in people put into situations and places no one person could possibly experience physically. In short, I wanted to embody life in the dance of language. I actually got started as a short story writer, but as I began to get into poetry I decided that what I wanted to do was write obviously good poems.

Masterson. What do you mean by that?

Turco. I mean poems that people could pick up and read and understand and enjoy, and that were obviously well-written.

Masterson. I'm still not quite sure what "obviously well-written" means. It's a very difficult thing to define, I'm sure.

Turco. It shouldn't be for anyone involved in teaching freshman composition. The writing should be well-structured and vivid, not private, not dense — that is, not opaque, though I wanted a textured poetry, certainly; textured thought and language.

Masterson. Who were some of your models then?

Turco. Very early, you mean?

Masterson. Yes.

Turco. One of my earliest pro-models was Edgar Allen Poe, oddly enough, perhaps. I loved Bryant's "Thanatopsis" — you know, when you're in grammar school and in high school (this is still true, perhaps) you read 19th century American Poetry — but I also read other people. I remember loving Walter de la Mare's "The Listeners." I loved a lot of Edwin Arlington Robinson. Of the later 20th century poets a little farther on, when I began to explore on my own, Dylan Thomas was paramount. He was a large influence on many people of my generation. Thomas, it seemed to me, had everything a poet ought to have.

Masterson. Didn't you find his poetry opaque?

Turco. I had no idea what he was talking about. I loved the way his poetry sounded. Later on, when I discovered that all he was saying was the standard Romantic things, it was a bit disillusioning; still, I loved the poetry. I began reading many of the moderns — E. E. Cummings, Vachel Lindsay, Edgar Lee Masters' *Spoon River Anthology*, early Eliot and Pound, Wallace Stevens, Robert Frost, Marianne Moore — that's a pretty catholic group, but what they all seemed to me to be interested in was writing obviously good poems, and that's what I wanted to do.

Masterson. You seem to write a great many things that are based on other texts.

Turco. That tends to be true for the series, not so much for the single poems. It takes me a long time to gather enough single poems for a collection, but a much shorter time to write a series. Yes, even *A Cage* *of Creatures* [1978] — which is a humanoid bestiary, by the way — is based mainly on Jorge Luis Borges' *The Book of Imaginary Beings* [1967], and each of the poems contains archaic words from Charles Mackay's *Lost Beauties of the English Language* [1874], so very early many of my influences were, and remain, literary. It tends to be things that I read that get me started writing my own work. Here's an example from *A Cage of Creatures*:

DYBBUK

It is in her eyes — the odd light,
and behind it a shadow, as though
　　someone were masked and helpless,
held captive and speechless. She moves

tautly. It is as if her flesh
were not her own: The muscles lag so
　　briefly one is hardly sure
they lag at all. The lips are hard

as agate; the cheeks are pallid;
the eyes hollow and blue. When she laughs,
　　the sound comes from far away,
sharp as an echo from a ledge.

The people in the room raise their
glasses and drink, uneasy at her
　　approach. They cannot hold her
gaze — the men shuffle, catch themselves;

the women smile like wire, for
there is no way to help. One must save
　　oneself first, furtively. One
must skime her from under lowered

Masterson. I see what you mean about the old words — "skime" is one, isn't it? But I understand it from the way you use it.

Turco. Yes, it's a word we've lost from the language, and we have to use a phrase to replace it: "glance at furtively." I put it in a context that I hoped would define it.

Masterson. Do you consciously attempt to distance yourself from your poem, to be objective about it during its composition, as in Eliot's idea of the "objective correlative"?

Turco. Yes, I do. But Eliot's invention of that term was making a large phrase out of a small idea. He was talking about seeing oneself in the world around one, and I believe in that, yes, I believe it's only possible for a person to define himself in terms of others. I think that one sees oneself most clearly mirrored in the people and things that surround one.

Masterson. So, no "confessional poetry" for you, then?

Turco. That doesn't mean I haven't written personal poetry — I have, and I don't object to "confession" so long as it sings. I think that what was wrong with a lot of confessional poetry of the 1960s was that it didn't sing. Most lyric poetry is confessional poetry, but what poets used to know is that one has to keep the reader interested in what one is saying. One of the earliest lessons I ever had in this regard was at the hands of an editor named Star Powers who ran *The American Poetry Magazine* back in the early 1950s. I had sent some young poems to her, and she wrote back and gave me good criticism. One of the things she said was that I ought to drop the "I" narrator. People don't care how the writer feels about something; they care about themselves, and they want to see themselves in the poems. That was an important lesson for me to learn. How can one keep the reader interested when one is talking specifically about oneself? The answer traditionally has been by means of interesting rhymes and singing meters. Singing confession is more interesting than yelling it in somebody's ear. Or one can distance oneself by substituting the third person "he" or "she" for the first person "I" and, in that distancing, allow the reader a chance to enter the poem vicariously and empathically.

I'm aware that people such as Robert Creeley believe that the egopoetic "I" is, in fact, more universal than any other viewpoint, and more inclusive, but I don't believe it. Whitman speaks exclusively for people who believe as he believes, and he doesn't convince those who don't see the world as he does. Certainly, he never spoke for me, not as far back as high school when I began reading his work along with that of the other 19th century poets.

Masterson. What I want to ask you now has to do with the question we've just finished. Do you consciously think about the demands your poetry places upon readers, and if that is the case, what sorts of readers do you have in mind when you write? Or do you write exclusively for yourself?

Turco. As I said earlier, I want to write obviously good poems, but as time goes by I discover that I have written what some might consider an obscure poem occasionally. That's not willful. When I'm writing I'm not consciously thinking of anything except what I'm doing right at that moment, on that sheet of paper. Getting the words right. One isn't thinking of some reader out there toward whom one is aiming the poem. At the same time, if one has had the conscious desire to write poetry that is understandable to other people, that has to be operating at some subliminal level. It's particularly in the rewriting of the poem that consideration would come into play: will the reader be able to understand this? As for instance when I used the word "skime" in "Dybbuk."

Masterson. Let me stop you here, because you've raised an important concern of mine — you're saying that, as the poet writes the poem initially, there is not much concern, if any, with an ideal idea of a reader?

Turco. No, I don't think so.

Masterson. But that, when you go back to it, however many times one does that, a concern with the audience arises?

Turco. Exactly. When a poem is finished sometimes someone may say, "I don't understand it." Then I'll perhaps go back and reconsider it because I'm disconcerted to find that I've written an obscure poem, never having intended to.

Masterson. You're saying that the poet has to accept the limitations of his audience at the very beginning?

Turco. I guess that's the answer to your question. When one is writing the poem, one is not aware of the audience, but the poet has already made a commitment to that audience before he ever starts to write any poem whatsoever. The audience Whitman intended to reach, supposedly, was the "common man," but it is not laborers and shopkeepers who read his poems; it's a literary audience, the same as for other poets, so he missed reaching the people for whom he ostensibly wrote. As for me, I'm not interested in reaching an audience that's into "rock poetry" or "visionary experience," for instance. I'm just not interested; it's not what I'm after. What I want to do is reach people who are fascinated, as I am, with the dance of language and with the human experience in its endless variety of forms.

Masterson. That would be evidenced by the fact that you're doing things with language through a number of your books that seem to me to place special kinds of demands on your readers — archaic words, complicated forms from previous centuries — which require a good deal of work from the reader, even an educated reader.

Turco. Well, I'm not doing much with complicated forms under my own name these days — I leave that to Wesli Court, but the kind of reader I'm after is the kind who is willing to invest some effort in reading the poem.

Masterson. I want to ask you about critics...poets and critics, because you yourself are both, as many contemporary poets are. Whom have you found to be the most helpful and perceptive critic of your own work, and do you think that poets make the best critics of poetry? And a third part of that question: must one be involved in the writing of poetry — whether he or she be amateur, professional, or agonist — in order to be a good critic?

Turco. Let's take the third part first: no, one does not need to write poetry in order to be a good critic. All one needs is a commitment to poetry, whether it's to writing it or reading it. Once a poem is written it belongs to the reader as much as to the writer; therefore, the reader has the right to say whatever he or she wants to about it.

As to the first part of your question, I feel that the critic who has best understood me in reviews or articles is Herbert R. Coursen, Jr., of Bowdoin College, but I wouldn't say he has "influenced" me. What he's done is to encourage me to believe that what I was attempting to do has in fact made an impact on a reader, so perhaps I've been at least partially successful in achieving my goal. And Coursen is himself a poet, so he would be perhaps an example of the ideal critic — one who is both a poet himself and a scholar — one who knows what a poet is trying to do and who has attempted to do it himself. Certainly, this sort of person would be likely to be the best sort of teacher of poetry writing.

Masterson. Do you feel that the conditions for the publication of poetry now in the U. S. are healthy?

Turco. There are multitudes of poets writing, but there are many magazines and presses publishing poetry as well. The one thing bad about the contemporary scene is that few of the major publishers are putting out much poetry. The so-called "alternative press" movement has taken up much of the slack, however. It's difficult to get things published because there's so much competition, but there are a lot of places to appear, and quite a few places in which young people may try their wings.

There are more poets writing today, and more little magazines and small presses publishing poetry, than ever before in the history of the world. Unfortunately, most of these publishers have limited distribution, so few readers see even a decent percentage of the material available. Certainly, writing and publishing poetry in America is flourishing.

Masterson. But is it healthier than it's ever been?

Turco. Definitely. But let's be clear — poetry is not popular; it's not even as popular as it was in 19th-century America. As I implied earlier, though, popularity is not necessarily a symptom of health for serious writing. After the Second World War the University of Iowa's Writers' Workshop spawned graduate and undergraduate writing programs all over the country, which helps to account for all the poets who are writing, and for the fact that their best audience is an academic one. It also helps to account for the little magazine and small press movements, which are founded and edited by those people who have gone through the writing workshops.

Every college in the country has at least one writing arts course, usually taught by a publishing writer. Writers weren't allowed to teach college before the War. Very seldom was there a writer on campus, and if there were one, he was present because he was a scholar also. But young people now are exposed to at least one writer on nearly every campus, and that can't be anything but healthy, it seems to me.

Masterson. You are a teacher and a poet; do you feel that these roles are complementary, mutually exclusive, or problematic in any way?

Turco. In my own case teaching is helpful. To get back to an earlier point — I'm not deeply interested, in a career sense, in anything but poetry, but one can't write poetry twenty-four hours a day, nor even twelve hours a day, nor, perhaps, even two hours every single day. It takes a great deal of mental labor and concentration to write poetry. But being involved with students who are interested in reading poetry and in writing it — being in an academic environment which is, perhaps, the only situation in which poetry is taken as a matter of course and treated as a serious occupation — is stimulating. There are other poets who won't teach at all because they find it debilitating, but I enjoy teaching as well as writing, and one has to eat, so it's lucky that I do.

Masterson. Yet, as you say, there are some poets who find it vitiating to talk about poetry, whether it is their own or not.

Turco. Yes. I think, though, that it's a good thing for young poets to have teachers who are publishing poets themselves to measure themselves against and to use as models. On the other hand, I find that the way poetry writing is taught on most campuses is deplorable.

Masterson. How so? How is it taught?

Turco. The teaching of poetry has been far too inductive since the 1960s when poets abandoned the teaching of craft and technique because the "Beats" equated formalism with militarism during the Vietnam War. It's incredible to me, but the teachers bought that nonsense and abandoned their responsibility as instructors and guides. They retained only their position as encouragers.

Unlike any other discipline on campus — as for instance music or graphic art — "creative writing" poetry professors do not teach basics. Instead, the poet comes into class, generally speaking, and encourages his students in whatever it is they're doing, and the teacher seldom discusses the elements of language art as it has been practiced through the long ages by the poets. I would like to see this situation change, and to a degree I think it is changing. Certainly, I know there are young people out there who want this kind of training — I receive letters, even phone calls from them. They are usually young people — on occasion not so young — who've come across *The Book of Forms* and who want to know where they can get more information about structure and craft.

Some of the reasons poets don't teach such things we have already talked about. Poets are superstitious; they are afraid that talking about craft is going to destroy the creative impulse. And quite a few of them prefer to play the role of guru rather than instructor. But, as I say to my students, "Just because you don't know what you're doing doesn't mean you're not doing it." And the corollary, "Know what you're doing so well that you don't have to think about it." That's what every good artist does. He or she learns craft so well that all one need do is concentrate on the creation of art. What we need is more real teachers of the craft in the workshops.

The writing of poetry is not a trivial occupation, nor is it an easy thing to learn how to make the language dance, and go deep. He who dedicates himself to these concerns is a true poet.

SHARING THE PATH OR CIRCUIT
OF THINGS THROUGH FORMS
Hyatt H. Waggoner

I

TO START OUT WITH AN IMPOSSIBLE METAPHOR and some euphuistic play, Lewis Turco's formalism, which he has both preached and practiced, has served him as both fur-lined greatcoat and stout club. As greatcoat it has provided protection against the cold winds of a season of the soul friendly only to snowmen. As club it has proved a witty and wicked weapon in Turco's attacks on neo-romantics like James Dickey for falling into the prophetic fallacy.

But enough of tropes and parody. The archaic flavor of "greatcoat" instead of "overcoat" and club instead of "death-rays" or some other weapon out of science fiction or present reality was meant to suggest that Turco as poet has tended to preserve and rework Modernist attitudes in our post-Modernist period, and Turco as critic has — how consciously I don't know — taken on the role of valiant defender of the timeless verities of the poet's art against all those who promote confusion by putting first what is properly secondary, for instance by writing "confessional" poetry or striking a "prophetic" stance. A poet, says Turco, is an "artificer" whose material is language. As he puts it at the beginning of "Defining the Poet" [originally published in *Concerning Poetry*, i:2, fall 1968 and reworked as Chapter 1 of his *Poetry: An Introduction Through Writing*, 1973], after contrasting the poet's "focus" with that of the fictionist, the dramatist, and the essayist, "We are left with the poet. What is his focus? What's left? There is nothing left but the *language* itself." [Turco's emphasis]. — "To the poet, language is a substance to be molded and shaped. All else is secondary." Immediately after this emphatic restatement of a "verity" — the poet as "maker" — at least as old as Aristotle, Turco has a little fun with its opposite number, the Platonic conception of the poet as prophet or seer who must be "beside himself" or "out of his mind" — the "method" of ecstasy — in order to write the highest kind of poetry: one of the rather confusing definitions of poetry to be found in the Oxford English Dictionary reads, "a writer in verse (or sometimes elevated prose) distinguished by imaginative power, insight, creativity, and faculty of expression." How does Oxford define elevated? — "raised up; at a high level. Also... exalted in character; lofty, sublime... elated... slightly intoxicated." That last definition is assumedly used in a jocular sense, but it is perhaps most to the point, for a good definition of a poet might be, "a writer who is intoxicated with language."

All this is still preliminary, not, certainly, to any attempt to settle for all time the question of which of these contrasting ideas of the poet is "true," or even "truer," though to be sure I find my own sympathies generally leaning somewhat toward the unfashionable Platonic notion — but to a discussion of the verse in *Awaken, Bells Falling* [1968] and a comparison of the poems in this volume with Turco's newest, as yet uncollected poems [published in 1973 as *The Weed Garden*]. What I am going to suggest is that right now, in Turco's latest poems, the effects of a warming trend in the poet's mental weather is evident, so that [*The Weed Garden*] may be expected to surprise those who have followed the newest poems as they have appeared in the magazines. The "new" Turco may well appear to be attired and equipped not with greatcoat and club but more in the fashion of Whitman, the "man on the road" as he describes himself in the opening lines of what would later be numbered section forty-six of "Song of Myself":

I know I have the best of time and space — and that I was never measured, and never will be measured.
I tramp a perpetual journey, (come listen all!)
My signs are a rain-proof coat, good shoes, and a staff cut from the woods...

II

Images of winter, of silence, and of either a cold darkness or a cold whiteness suggest, and sometimes establish, the prevailing mood of *Awaken, Bells Falling*. Quite often they seem to echo early Stevens or early Frost, or both at once. In the title poem the climactic passage in "The Whiteness of the Whale" in *Moby-Dick* is, consciously or unconsciously, drawn upon to enrich the suggestions of the images. Reading "Winter; / allcolor; whiteness...." we can't help remembering how Melville put it: the whiteness of the perpetual arctic snow was "the colorless all-color of atheism." When we read the final lines of the poem— "Bells fail in the streets; / the hall empties us into ice, / sheeted, sheer as mirrors, unreflecting." — we find ourselves in the not too different world of Stevens, who thought one must have a mind of winter to survive.

"Letter to W.D.S" suggests one of the reasons why Turco finds a certain reticence preferable to the "confessional" poet's baring of the soul ("Why did you flay yourself there, in the / marketplace?"):

All of us are
alone. The world we blow through is cold.
Snow fetters our sorrow. Still we flute and fife.

In "The Burning Bush" the angel at the top of the Christmas tree does not light up when it should, nor any voice speak, though, like Frost in "For Once, Then, Something...," "...for a moment / he thought that the bush had / started to speak." Instead, the only epiphany comes from "cold stars," "a wind he had not heard / nor wished to hear," and "snow." In "The Forest of My Seasons" — a disguised sestina, the only traditionally formal piece in this volume of syllabic poems — the speaker adjures the dreaming part of himself to dream of "winter's hunting horns / blown to silence. Dream no longer of snow...." One reason for trying not to dream of it any more is that for today's poet it is too easy:

THE FOREST OF MY SEASONS

Desire today is a cavern of snow;
ice rimes all limbs with synonyms for wind.
Yesternoon it was goat-time, time for horns
rampant on a field *vert* under the woods
quartered in a southern compass. Toucan
tones rose close beneath the surface of shade,

threatening rupture. Poet, draw your shade
today upon a mirror made of snow
shadowed. Men may hibernate if bears can.
Desire must sleep in a cavern of wind
till it may be harried awake by wood-
pecker beak and Pan's sunsharp or ramshorns —

Too many words, like girdles built of horn,
confined in an attic. How to say *shade*
but make it mean more, as: tiles of the wood
laid for light to walk on; and to have snow
imply more than God's linoleum. Wind
is wind, but direction matters. Who can

help me? Where's my muse today? Shake your can,
you errant Echo, and get home. My horns
sprout long as the cuckoo's song while you wind
your own clock and make love with your own shade
someplace up a cavern or down the snow
where wild Narcissus buds among your woods.

The grows strange woods
sometimes; this fall of words grows as it can,
not as it ought. My pen is cold as snow:
its ink runs like chilled honey from the horns
of silence. Lie you down, lie down in shade,
word-warbler. Sleep sound with your mistress wind.

And while you sleep, dream. Dream of the south wind
needling you awake with slivers of woods:
birch and pine, maple that sweetens in shade;
oak on the white hillside. Dream, if you can,
of gray moles, brown mice, winter's hunting horns
blown to silence. Dream no longer of snow,

for time and flesh shall do more than wind can
to blend your words with woodwinds and woodshorns.
There will be tonics. It's time for shades now.

How does one flute and fife in such weather? Like this, for instance,
again from the title poem:

AWAKEN, BELLS FALLING

It is a dawn quick as swallows
        peeling to shear through peals belled
    from the one town steeple. Autumn
    falls from green heat like a chestnut felled
out of its prickly jacket. A single

    jay walks in the pines. A cone of
        cold sweeps chill's needles soughing
    through the day's screen doors. There can be
    no cushioning today: to wake
shall be a sharp thing. The person on his

private ticking will be palsied
from his sheets, his numeral
be rung, the coils of consciousness
spring him into good woolen light,
without armament, to meet himself in

mirrors and still halls. Meet himself —
find his blood walking a thin
line, alarums unsleeping him.
Brazen as flame leaving ash for
the elm's sere leaf, autumn will have settled

into summer's pallet — patchwork
and quilting: that poor thread of
dreams curling at the doorsill. It
is done, the keen tone spoken, wrung
out of the bronze tongue of silence. Winter;

allcolor; whiteness. Who will braid
our years now into what skein
of circles? Bells fail in the streets;
the hall empties us into ice,
sheeted, sheer as mirrors, unreflecting.

In so cold and threatening a world as Turco inhabits in this book
artifice can be both shield and weapon, or greatcoat and club. For me,
though, the finest poem in the volume shows much less of that "easy
virtuosity" that August Derleth [see bibliography, below] called attention to in a review. It is not primarily such verbal play as we have in the
lines just quoted that gives "Burning the News" its power:

BURNING THE NEWS

The fire is eating
the paper. The child who drowned
is burned. Asia is in flames.
As he signs his great
bill, a minister of state chars

at the edges and curls
into smoke. The page rises,
glowing, over our neighbor's
roof. In the kitchens
clocks turn, pages turn like gray wings,

slowly, over armchairs.
Another child drowns, a bill
is signed, and the pen blackens.
The smoke of Asia
drifts among the neighbors like mist.

It is a good day for burning.
The fire is eating the news.

There is nothing euphuistic about lines like "The smoke of Asia / drifts among the neighbors like mist." Where does its power come from? From the vision behind and in the words, perhaps?

Modesty ought to, and ordinarily would — or if not modesty, the desire to maintain the appearance of it — forbid me to talk as I am about to of my latest book [*American Poets from the Puritans to the Present*, 1968] and its effect on Turco. But the poet himself has already put the story in print in his review of the book ["The Ghost of Emerson or, No Use Trying to Keep Away from Spirits"] ("...it's not a review, but a response") in *The Carleton Miscellany* [x:1, Winter 1969, pp. 99-104], and to leave it out here for good taste's sake or any other sake would make it impossible to talk meaningfully about the change in Turco's work going on right now, the change that made me predict in the beginning that his next book [*The Weed Garden*] will surprise his readers. The title he gives his non-review, "The Ghost of Emerson," refers both to a claim made by and the organizing idea in my book — roughly, Emerson's centrality in the development of American poetry — and to Turco's own personal "response." Like Eliot meeting the ghost of Dante during the London blitz, Turco encountered the ghost of Emerson and came to think of the encounter as a revelation, or series of revelations.

Since the bulk of his review is made up of excerpts from the letters with which, for several months, he bombarded me, the best thing I can do here, I guess, is to let him explain the matter in his own words, stressing the "response" aspect and omitting the flattering evaluations of the book:

> *American Poets* happened to appear at a time when I was confused about a good many things, and it cleared up many of my confusions. It made me see much about poetry starkly for the first time, and it helped me to understand myself better, myself and some of the things I have been groping toward as a writer.

* * * *

Two things emerge...in the book. First, we see in perspective the warring in America between Makers and Sayers as each point of view attempts to dominate the scene. Second, we see, as in Emerson himself, that most major American poetry, especially in the twentieth century, is part of an immense religious and philosophical debate — among mechanists, humanists, various kinds of romantics, existentialists, hedonists, evangelists, traditional religionists — which continues into the present.

* * * *

As I read the book and began to see these things, I got very excited. Whole valleys of fog began to burn off, and vistas of American poetic history opened up to me, vistas no other book I know of has been able to shed light upon. And here are excerpts of the letters I began to write to Hyatt H. Waggoner:

Forgive me for bombarding you like this, but I am reading your book, and it is having a tremendous effect on me. I might as well be reading the Bible: day after day of revelations. That must sound florid, but it is nevertheless true. You are speaking straight to me, and it doesn't even matter if you think I am a whack and do not answer my letters.

Until I got into your book I had a personality as badly split as Williams. The amazing thing about your book is not that it finally explains all of American poetry to me, but that it also explains myself to me, and when I finished the chapter on Eliot and saw, at last, that our 20th century poetry is in effect a huge religious debate — saw, further, what it was the poets were debating about, I realized the nature of the debate that was going on inside me, underneath, and the terror of my conscious mind because of my refusal to understand or work out the loss of my own religion — or, rather, that of my father, who is a minister and who, I now realize, is closer to the place I've finally come than I would ever have been willing to admit before I read *American Poets* [cf. *The Spiritual Autobiography of Luigi Turco*, edited, with an introductory memoir, by Lewis Turco for the Center for Immigration Studies at the University of Minnesota, Ann Arbor: University Microfilms O-P Books, 1969].

* * * *

I read Emerson's essay "The Poet" last night and today. Amazing.

* * * *

I'm not against vision. It's just that I've never had any that I could identify as such.

* * * *

If I don't have vision, in the mystical sense, I do have a "long view," like Loren Eiseley.

* * * *

Another thing, since I read your book and saw these things, I don't fear death as once I did.

* * * *

Another thing your book did: it has stopped me from writing very much. I'm incapable now, I think, of writing... "pleasances."...

* * * *

Man is Nature attempting to understand itself, someone said; minds will one day become Mind.

* * * *

I have finished writing this review, and I am sitting here staring at that last sentence. Does it seem to have a vague, slightly frightening Emersonian quality about it? Or is that just my imagination again?

III

Along with the flood of letters there came every now and then a copy of a new poem, several directly inspired by passages in [*American Poets*], others showing the influence the poet himself has described. An example of the former type is "Mary Moody Emerson, R.I.P.," which strikes me as a finer poem than anything in *Awaken* with the possible exception of "Burning the News":

MARY MOODY EMERSON, R. I. P.
for Hyatt H. Waggoner

Ralph Waldo's Aunt Mary,
moody as all getout, got herself
   rigged out in a shroud and rode
   through Concord on a donkey
"to get herself in the habit of the

tomb." Ralph Waldo, though she
wore her cerements daily ever
   after, reckoned her beast of
   burden was more symbolic
than her garb. If he could transcend Calvin,

concordantly, why not
she? Ceremonies of Innocence
   and Hope lay everywhere before her grave step, were she but
to look: "There grow the *Leaves of Grass*." But what

makes them so green? "On the
village square a concourse of elms praises
   the good Lord." In their shadow
   the moss grows. "All are Elect!"
Then why so few who can see? Ralph Waldo

shrugged and put down to whim this
relative moodiness. When they put
   her down at last in her life-
   long weeds, Ralph Waldo blessed her
blind eyes as, no doubt, Aunt Mary blessed his.

Two examples of the latter sort are "I Am Peter" and "The Pilot." The former looks inward:

I AM PETER

I am Peter,
the original rock. On me
all churches are founded.
I gave my substance to be joined with water

that all this world's
things might have their being, even
flesh and dust. I am no
man, but am half of All. Out of the night

that moves through time
like a spider without a face;
out of suns like needles
that are the spider's eyes, I move with my fluid

wife. Our motion
is a begetting of motion.
I do not think; water
does not feel. Yet I will sire thought out of

waves, under night,
and light shall be woven into
the fabric of being.
The penultimate son will understand that

I am Peter;
his child will understand I Am.
He will be the thinking
Rock, the feeling Wave — flesh, dust, heart, mind, Maker.

The latter looks outward:

THE PILOT

Calais, France, May 18, 1968 (AP) — Low tide yesterday uncovered a plane, presumably of World War II, with the remains of the pilot still at the controls. Its origin could not be determined immediately.

It has been
a long flight. Like flak,
the seagrass exploded
beneath me as I fell
    out of light into
an older and a heavier air.

My planing
continued in the tide.
When the scavengers had
done with my flesh, I found
    that still the stick would
answer, though more slowly than before.

So I flew,
and am flying still, back
to the beginning. In
my marrow direction
    lay. Now the sea has
released me, and I have been constant.

But I was
wrong. You see me at death's
controls, in the primal
mud where our flight began,

but it has not been
a fleeing, as we have long supposed.

I see that
now, with these sockets where
fish have swum. You, rising
from the shore, have shown me
what the snail tried to
tell: the journey is the other way.

Turn me around. I am with you still.

"Looks": I mean it as an allusion to Emerson's favorite metaphor for the power that makes the poet a Seer.

The true poet, Emerson thought, "looks" through a "transparent eyeball" (all defenses down, screening out nothing, admitting all, but "looking," of course, from the proper "angle of vision") both inward and outward, not necessarily all at once. "Dante's praise is, that he dared to write his autobiography in colossal cipher, or into universality." But also, the poet's "insight, which expresses itself by what is called Imagination, is a very high sort of seeing, which does not come by study, but by the intellect being where and what it sees, by sharing the path or circuit of things through forms, and so making them translucid to others." And finally — from "Circles" this time instead of from "The Poet": "...so to be is to know."

"I Am Peter" is a very personal, very autobiographical, poem — to one who knows the poet's circumstances — while still avoiding the "confessional" qualities Turco has so often said he despised. It is also, it seems to me, a very fine and moving poem, some miles along the road beyond most if not all of the earlier work.

Both the poem on Emerson's Aunt Mary and "The Pilot" seem to me to exemplify Emerson's idea of the poetic imagination, which suggests, among other modern variants, Buber's notion of "dialogue" —

an "I-Thou" relation, made possible only by imagination and will, to use the old terms, rather than an "I-It" form of scrutinizing. In "The Pilot," especially, the poet's "angle of vision" has changed and he is really, it seems to me, doing what Emerson meant by "sharing the circuit of things through forms," making the "forms translucid," so the light can shine through.

I shall have to let just these two poems suffice to illustrate what I have been saying about "the new Turco" just now coming into poetic (And personal? Emerson would insist that it must be so.) being. Just one further remark on it: notice how much less purely verbal glitter there is in this poem than in the already quoted opening lines of the title poem of *Awaken*: and yet, as it seems to me at least, there is more light, of several sorts.

To any reader who happens to agree that "The Pilot" shows us a growing poet who has already moved a good way beyond the average level of his achievement in *Awaken*, who has come to the point where he no longer needs the greatcoat and the club, let me say only this: that if Lewis Turco really is, as I think, no longer "hung up" as a poet by many of the same insoluble problems that hung up Stevens, whom in *Awaken* he so often echoes, if he is moving [in *The Weed Garden*] far beyond "an easy virtuosity," then Emerson did it. As old-fashioned theological orthodoxy would have it, my book served as "an unconscious agent of Grace."

But that's good enough for me, and for Turco too I should guess. I don't think he'll mind my liking his newest work better than his earlier "pleasances."

IV

Turco's 1985 collection *The Compleat Melancholick* is identified as "Being a Sequence of Found, Composite, and Composed Poems, based largely upon Robert Burton's *The Anatomy of Melancholy*." I've been picking it up and browsing in it almost every day since it arrived, rather than reading it straight through at once — it seemed to invite that kind of approach.

The book as a whole is an interesting experiment, and I've enjoyed the time I've spent with it. There are many reasons for being melancholy, but this book is not one of them. Rather, it seems to distance the reasons and hold the melancholy at bay, partly by its relation to Burton's book, partly by Turco's own — sometimes quite dark — humor:

THE COMPLEAT MELANCHOLICK
out of Burton

"Of seasons of the year,
the Autumn is most melancholy."
Then lovers lie within their sheets,
thoughts winding among their separations,
dreaming of darknesses chill enough
"to refrigerate the heart —

"windy melancholy,"
cholick of leaves and limbs, of owlcry
and blue hound moaning at the sky.
"Some persons think that every star's a world,
and call this earth of ours an obscure
star, presided over by the least of

"gods." The lovers dream of
"phrenzy, ecstasy, revelations,
visions, enthusiasms," these
demons of the blood. "The Talmudists say
that Adam had a wife called Lilis,
before he married Eve, &

"of her he begat no
Thing but Dyvils. These unclean spirits
            settled in our bodies, and now
mixed with our melancholy humours, do
        triumph as it were, and sport themselves
            as in another heaven.

                "Cauls, kells, tunicles, creeks"
are their changelings for our desires. "By
            their charms they can draw down the moon
from the heavens." The lovers? — they lie to
wish. "This humour of Melancholy
            is called the Devil's Bath." You

                least of Gods, this is
a petty Hell: These solitary
            pallets beneath the falling moon.
I conjure you, with little charm, "Bring their
sweethearts to them by night, upon a
            goat's back flying in the air."

THE PROGRESS OF LEWIS TURCO
William Heyen

THE INHABITANT (1970) IS THE COLLECTION OF POEMS that Lewis
Turco has been heading toward for a long time. As his books have
appeared his work has not only gotten better, but has changed. A poet
can get better while his way of seeing — I am talking about something
as elusive as vision — does not change. Near the end of his life Robert
Frost said he still believed what he believed sixty years before, that his
beliefs hadn't changed. This makes for emotional comfort, to be sure,
but probably not for excellence. To read Frost's *Collected Poems* is to
realize that he is incredibly over-rated, and by some of our best poets —
Kinnell, Snodgrass, Wilbur, Meredith. The sensibility behind Frost's
work delimits it. He does not achieve, or perhaps even aspire, to
dramatic intensity. He achieved, early, a symbolic speech that he could
not or at least did not consolidate before going on. To read Cleanth
Brooks in *Modern Poetry and the Tradition on Frost* is to nod agreement
sadly. But this is all a long story. Wallace Stevens called poetry a
"supreme fiction" and said that one of the things the fiction had to do
was change.

I

Most of the work in Turco's *First Poems* (1960) is too stiff
metrically, or too pretty, or too ingenious, or too heavily moral and
wise. Depending on your tolerance for "promising" first volumes, you're
likely to consider Turco's apprentice work "very pleasant to hear," as did
Donald Justice when he wrote a Foreword for *First Poems*, or as merely
a sort of unpromising game "exhibiting the most ordinary of all kinds
of skill," as did James Dickey when he reviewed it. Dickey most

99

objected to Turco's seeming to try out every damn verse form there is — he has, in fact, in *The Book of Forms: A Handbook of Poetics* (1968), indexed them — and Justice's seeming to condone these Tarzanian exploits. What most concerns me here is the strenuous and irritating morality of the book, something the poet had to grow out of. Nothing is more aggravating in poetry than the presentation of conventional wisdom unless it is the presentation of conventional wisdom conventionally. It is not just that some of Turco's early poems are didactic, poems of statement, poems with some of the excesses of newspaper obituary verse, but that behind them is a sort of puritanical fury that demands that every action, everything that happens to anyone at any time anywhere should and must yield its drop of meaning. Meaning everywhere, but not a drop to think. Turco wasn't willing to allow a poem to well up from its own subtle sense of itself, wasn't willing to allow it to do what it wanted to do.

In any case, apprentice work, it seems to me, does become interesting as its potential is or is not fulfilled with more mature poems, and this is reason enough for its publication. Though, as Herman Melville said, of all the insignificant things in the world a poet's first book is the most, a poet's development is the development of spirit, and there is nothing that should be more important to us. The protean Theodore Roethke — Stanley Kunitz calls him a poet of transformations — made every volume new again. It is the great split in Eliot's career that fascinates us. The poet as hero struggles, reaches. Frost and Cummings repeated themselves tiresomely. A poet who does not change is writing out of habit and echo and imitation of an old self. Frost thought it admirable to remain constant. No. And the poems themselves will reveal the depth of the sensibility that brought them into being.

So, as long as early poems are better than the blank page, good enough. I want to see them and read them alongside later ones. They are a test. W. H. Auden said that if you look at two poems by the same poet and can't tell which was written first he's a minor poet. At the same time, any undue pride in the initial gropings of early work is, of course, unbearable, but there's no trouble here: my copy of *First Poems* is inscribed by Turco "with apologies for most of these."

II

Awaken, Bells Falling: Poems 1959-1967 (1968) represents a great step forward. This third collection — an impossible-to-get-hold-of chapbook, *The Sketches*, was published in 1962 — has already arrived. Most of the poems are finished and satisfying. Occasionally the sermonic tone of *First Poems* still breaks through and is offensive, but for the most part skill, awareness, and curiosity brought these poems into being rather than the constant puritanical rage for a sign. Turco's voice is less insistent. Authorial intrusion is at a minimum. The sensibility behind these poems has made an intelligent decision, a decision of the intelligence, and is willing to allow its subjects to Be rather than constantly Become. An example of the book's method and belief is its shortest poem, "School Drawing":

SCHOOL DRAWING

There is a road: no
one is walking there. Brown
paper, black paper triangles
wrangle with the air
to make a windmill

striping a crayon
sun. A black arrow points
away from the blades that turn in
fire. It is burning,
and there is no wind.

This means what it says, no more and no less. Turco has gone back to the innocence of words here. The fire of illumination in this book, as in "School Drawing" and "Burning the News," burns up the old ways we've had of bringing a scaffolding of meaning to a poem. The crutches are in flames, says Turco. Poems dwell on the edge of mystery. "There is a road: no / one is walking there." The subject of this poem is the Being of the drawing, not what Turco thinks it means or what I think it means. Turco is now willing to allow his subject to surface when and how it pleases. He is willing to suggest rather than state. He has gotten past trying to prove anything. And this kind of poem, I must insist, is neither flippant nor shallow. It is motivated, in Turco at least, by a complex of emotional needs, some of which I hope to suggest before I'm done talking here.

His poems in this third collection, then, are aware of themselves as bearers of consciousness, awareness, intelligence, but are not as strident or methodical or militant as *First Poems*. The poems now, in fact, are metaphors for what seems to be a developing vision. Poetry now, as he writes in ["A Dedication"] to John Malcolm Brinnin and Donald Justice, who would know, "explains why / ...even as it explains nothing." I don't think Turco realized the complexity of this truth during the time *First Poems* was being forced into shape. In "An Immigrant Ballad" from his first book the poet describes his own father being caught by Jesus, "nailed...by the throat." One of the times a poem is not a poem is when it is metrical theology, and it is the minister's son who is clearly in evidence behind Turco's early poems. But not by the time of *Awaken*. In a 1969 interview [published as "Craft and Vision," edited by David G. McLean, in *The DeKalb Literary Arts Journal* [iv: 4, 1970, pp. 1-14] Turco said, "I don't believe that there has been a God that has created everything. I feel that maybe the earth and the entire universe are evolving Godhead through its creatures, one of whom is man. And one of the ways in which Godhead evolves is by an individual's being conscious of the earth, being conscious of the universe, being conscious of itself." Turco goes on to define the place that intelligence has in poetry: "And consciousness implies intelligence, which is one of the reasons why I feel intelligence cannot be denied in poetry. 'It is the world trying to know itself,' I think somebody said."

What is missing here, and happily so, is the sense of absolutism one gets when reading the earlier poems. Now the universe and its creator, or the principles that make it move and change as it does, are seen as great mysteries toward which words, not the word, can edge. To throw the gates of awareness, of consciousness wide open, to intuit and control at once — this is the way. In "The Late, Late Show," Turco suggests that when we perceive the end (of the universe or of a poem) too clearly, it no longer really matters.

III

I don't quite know how to put this, but what I feel reading *The Inhabitant* (1970) is a deep and strong sense of my own existence, my own loneliness in time. The twenty-eight poems — "The Hallway," "The Couch," "The Kitchen," "The Pillow," "The Mirror," "The Study" are typical   titles — dramatize the Inhabitant's developing consciousness of his domestic world in terms that are near and clear. Images of emptiness, absence, loss, boredom, fatigue, monotony, darkness, stagna-tion, and corrosion dominate. But Turco turns so much domestic dross into poetry, and the effect of this book is strangely uplifting. The poems are a record of a nameless man's willingness to allow his world to be.

In *The Inhabitant* Turco moves to a concept of the "still-point"not as the fruition of a life of mystical straining or as one of the strange momentary joys of our lives, but as a necessity, a defensive gesture, our minds defending us, against ourselves, as Stevens says in one of his "Adagia." In "The Forest Beyond the Glass" from *Awaken*, a poem that images two bull moose in a museum display still locked together by their horns as they had been found after combat, one with a broken neck and one that later died of thirst, Turco writes, "But it was not /

103

love that had / conquered; as usual, it was / time." In "The Playroom" from *The Inhabitant* Turco returns to the moose again, but because the Inhabitant's daughter says to him that she wishes she were nothing since then nothing could hurt her, he realizes that for him Time the Destroyer must become Time the Creator. The Inhabitant tries to convince himself to "forget the moose: they'd had a lovely life, free and roaming the free mountains, water falling in the great gorge, wind in their horns, their loins and lungs bursting with love — forget the moose. He tells his daughter, who cannot forget the moose behind glass, that he will not let "Jack, old Time, the giant killer," hurt her. He says to us then, and to himself, "If these be lies, they are but slight distortion." He vows "to make his pallet on the book of hurts," and to blind time should it "slither out" from the pages to grab hold of his daughter. "Or he will wink and blind her with his love." This would require, of course, a major readjustment of the concept of time, both for himself and for his daughter. The word "wink" comes from Stevens' "A High-Toned Old Christian Woman": "But fictive things / Wink as they will. Wink most when widows wince." Now, wishing for the happiness of his young and probably godless daughter, he is determined to be her star, her center, something like "the stars winking in at the windows, lying about where they were in the night by light years and by dark," something like Williams" star in "El Hombre" and Stevens' star in "Nuances of a Theme of Williams," a fictional star that will blind her to the realities of time and death with love.

"The Playroom" is a deep and rewarding poem. It takes the Inhabitant's awareness into the moving realm of his relationship with his daughter. "The Portrait of a Clown," which follows "The Playroom" — both poems are spatially, technically, and thematically at the dead center of the book — is a companion piece, a sequel. It again poses the questions unresolved by "The Playroom": how can the Inhabitant be his child's world? how can he save her from pain? how can he make his own world suffice?

The answer is not programmatic or definite, but the Inhabitant is on the verge of knowing, and I am too. I must quote the poem:

THE PORTRAIT OF A CLOWN*

Which way will he go
for his lips
are at the edge of something

shades of blue rose-flushed
it is a
pavilion on the green wall silk

and canvas and the wall
is on the
edge of something the room is

hanging on the lip of
evening neither starward
nor sunward how will the clown

maintain his equipoise as a
world as a
room tips the frame tilts shades

of aquamarine the bold lines
of a face
ride over the sleeping child.

Somehow, he must become a room "hanging on the lip of / evening neither starward / nor sunward...." Consciousness has to be adjusted to the present. He'll make himself over first, be a clown of equipoise. And from here on the Inhabitant is intent on capturing the stillness that is real, now, the moment you are reading this. If the objects are symbolically extended forward and backward in time, if the Inhabitant's mind is still at play, he senses that he is indulging himself. If the universe is evolving, changing, there is a sense in which it is, at any moment, during any one day of total consciousness, deathless, as still in time as Zeno's paradoxical arrow.

The Inhabitant's struggle (and, since we seem to enter "The Door" in the first poem, ours) is to accept his world and to become his own "true flesh," as Turco puts it. The seventh and last section of "The Dwelling-House," a prose poem that ends the volume, concludes:

> He went to the door, naked; opened it; moved into the daylight where the world walked. With his eyes he met other eyes beyond the portal — men, women and children who knew his nakedness as he knew theirs.

> It was a true flesh the Inhabitant made to walk through the city: in each eye he saw the image folk saw in his.

After making the world, after six days and several dreams, it is time to walk naked, beyond dream. Part V of this poem begins: "On the fifth day the Inhabitant awoke and saw that God was dead." Turco's poem is a summary of where he has come from. As it ends it recalls Stevens in "Final Soliloquy of the Interior Paramour":

> We say God and the imagination are one...
> How high that highest candle lights the dark.

> Out of this same light, out of the central mind,
> We make a dwelling in the evening air,
> In which being there together is enough.

For Stevens, of course, the old gods were dead and poetry had to take their places. The happy thing in Stevens is that men could experience "the heavenly fellowship / Of men that perish" ("Sunday Morning"), that "being there together is enough." And this is where Turco takes us, to an eye-to-eye contact with one another, naked together, naked, unsponsored and free. Stephen Crane (whose funeral Stevens attended) drew that lost world particularly clearly in "The Open Boat," a story that strips away illusions of sponsorship. But even if the Creator or First Cause or whatever was the kind of artist who brought forth a gull that looked as though it were hacked out with a jackknife, even though the understanding that came from the correspondent's immersion in the destructive element is dark, the men in the boat draw closer together despite, in fact because of their existential dilemma.

And one other analogy is important here: Crane's story and Stevens' poems, though we could expect the opposite, move toward, rather than chaos and amorality, a humanistic morality. Crane's correspondent, feeling that death is imminent and in sight of an uncaring universe, still wishes that he had lived differently and that he had a chance to mend his life; Stevens senses a "planet's encouragement" for us to make this only life the finale of our desires. Loss of faith does not necessarily lead to nihilism.

The Inhabitant walks from attic to cellar of his home listening to his furniture declare its own plain songs. As was Roderick Usher, the Inhabitant is hypersensitive and feels the sentience of all things. But the House of Usher, of course, disappears under the tarn of time; Turco's house seems, finally, to flourish in the here and now, something Poe always despised.

Stevens said that the greatest poverty was not to live in a physical world. In "The Porch" Turco's Inhabitant walks down the street to witness the aftermath of an automobile accident. After the spectators leave, Turco enters his protagonist's mind:

> Some of the crowd will dream; therefore, the Inhabitant shall
> stay awake upon the porch to work by lamplight upon his

cards — ordering his neighbors' names, memorizing the streets of towns, listening to June bloom again and to a cat greeting another dawn.

He wants to fix his time, order it. His effort is... to love, to love the dark and beautiful contingency of his experience. Yves Bonnefoy quotes Hegel: "Now the life of the spirit does not cringe in front of death nor keep itself pure from its ravage. It supports death and maintains itself on it." And in "The Bedroom" (an adaptation from the French of Bonnefoy's "A Shadow Breathing") the Inhabitant knows that this vision of life is natural and true: "a pagan peacock flaunts its mortal raiment."

"The Cat" becomes for the Inhabitant a symbol of "the palpable dark." It knocks a pen out of his hand and insists on being "stroked and enjoyed for / it is lethal and sensual / as well and it means / no particular ill." Well, I have been too concerned with Idea here, with Turco's movement toward that world, beyond the explanations of old gods, where the Inhabitant comes to stillness and joy. This spiritual progress, I take it, is part of what Conrad Aiken means when he calls *The Inhabitant* a poetry of "whole meaning." This book is a whole world, not a slice of life, and one of the fascinating things about where Turco's break with his past has taken him is that the world he has opened for himself is dynamic, self-propagating, endless. There are numberless things that Turco can now allow to be themselves. (In *Images or Shadows of Divine Things* Jonathan Edwards is indeed ingenious in draining metaphysical meaning from almost everything — our tongues are hidden behind our teeth because our speech must be guarded — but I wonder if even he could have done anything with the appliances in Turco's "The Kitchen.") It seems to me that this is a good test of any aesthetic, any world view: can it take everything into account?

Anyway, I have worried too much about Idea, about the assumptions of *The Inhabitant*. Many of the poems here are wonderfully realized, satisfied with themselves, not straining to be more, finished.

The perceptions of many are deeply intelligent and moving. This is "The Couch":

THE COUCH

It waits against
the wall like some
old lion couching in gloom

it is harmless
one can be seated
on its hide and it

will not move
even to take its
repast look one may be

seated here and
one will not disappear
into the plush flowers that

camouflage hunger it
is harmless though famished
in the room on the

carpet which rolls
into the underbrush of
an evening murmurous with crickets.

I like this way of seeing. The Inhabitant's metaphor is playful. Even as he spins his jungle and lion analogy he realizes that the couch's couchness is inviolate, that a lot of songs could accompany the singular miracle of its existence. The whole point is that this book is the creation of the Inhabitant and is itself the realization of his success in yoking

Time to the present, making a dynamic and joyful and pure presentness of things present, casting suspicion on human memory and symbol-making that leads to despair. There is a sense in which Turco has gone back, through darkness to a condition of affirmation.

In one poem Stevens calls metaphor a lion; in another, light is a lion that comes down to drink. If Turco's "An Ordinary Evening in Cleveland" from *Awaken* is a cynical answer to Stevens" "An Ordinary Evening in New Haven," answering, as it does, Stevens' high spirits with depression and sterility, "The Couch" and other poems in *The Inhabitant* are manifestations of a new faith in the meaningfulness of the mental and physical worlds.

*An early painting by Tomie DePaola, the children's writer and illustrator, a classmate of Turco and his wife, Jean, at Meriden High School in Connecticut 1949-52. As co-editor of *The Annual, 1952*, Turco was the first publisher of the work of DePaola, who was the art editor for the yearbook.

WHOLE MEANING AGAIN
by Herbert R. Coursen, Jr.

Lewis Turco has been called a "poet's poet," and that is truly what he is, a craftsman who weighs each word in the palm of his mind, knowing which word will work, and which word will not. The effect of a Turco poem is, "These words and no others." The individual poems are invariably of high quality, a quality especially remarkable when one considers the virtually complete range of formal approaches that Turco employs. His is a virtuosity which only Auden, perhaps, among modern poets, can match. When Turco writes a series of poems, as he has often done (beginning with *The Sketches* in 1962), and as he has done in these books, the effect easily exceeds the sum of the parts.

I

To discuss *The Inhabitant* is to do the book an immediate injustice, like translating into the fragmentation of language the meaning of an experience which has meant what it has meant. The book should be read like a novel, beginning with the first poem, "The Door," and expanding with the Inhabitant as he haunts his rooms looking for the self that became — before he was aware — his own ghost. Lewis Turco's *The Inhabitant* emerges from the consciousness of a man searching the rooms of his house, listening to the footfalls of his heart until, in the last poem, "The Dwelling House" — a modern allegory of Creation — he gradually unwinds himself from his dream and walks naked through his city, knowing that "in each eye he saw the image folk saw in his." That final reflection of and from the eyes of humanity is the Inhabitant's inheritance from the myriad reflecting surfaces and reflective rooms of his house.

To open the doors of this house is to enter rooms animated by their own life. Suddenly the word livingroom takes its stress on the last syllable, as its "Lamps dimly recall old shadows in the various corners." This is the dimension we expect — and sometimes find — in poetry, the reverberation beneath the seemingly simple surface. In "The Livingroom" the Inhabitant confronts his former self, the young skull beneath the aging flesh, his youth reflected to him, imagery of death:

> He watches the skull grow upward on its stem of spine; he waits
> till it is tall as a lily, and the chairs wait, the couches roar
> quietly.

In "The Attic" the Inhabitant visualizes "mirrors reflecting upon solitude." Life may move below the attic, but the attic itself is alive:

> The mathoms listen
> until, downstairs, carpets swallow the noises of living, until the
> furniture absorbs motion.

> Then the machine clicks on: the clock dial begins to turn; dust
> feeds the cogs. It is making things, making them slowly, out
> of the debris of afternoons and the streetlamp suicides of
> evening moths.

Downstairs, the Inhabitant senses "a vague weightfulness overhead," but only his pet understands, "and, now and then, the cat acts strangely." Things are alive up there, in the dust and the dark.

"The Cat" receives a poem of its own, imaged as "lethal but sensual," an inoffensive pet that echoes the malevolence of its wild relatives. This cat is "a familiar of houses," not of witches, "a domestic that keeps accounts," but that touches the edge of darker metaphors, realized in "The Couch," which "waits against / the wall like some / old lion couching in gloom." The familiar fuses with the image of a huge cat, hungry behind the jungle flowers — but the metaphor cannot be paraphrased, must be felt as it evolves within the poem.

"The Hallseat" holds in breathless mimesis the process of autumn, the golden oak fading the

> paper fading behind a
> spotted mirror

and holds the past within its impress:

> only in the seat itself
> where certain moments repose
> forgotten now

The hallseat must sit against its wall and wait for someone to tumble into memory.

"The Photograph" suggests that "it is unwise / to trap a moment such as this / in a frame gilt or / otherwise," yet captures the inexplicable process of growing old in a way that can only be felt deeply within the relationship between the poem and its reader. To quote it in bits and pieces is to try to trap a moment, to lie about the way it means.

"The Glider" on the porch, reminiscent of so many summers past, becomes a vehicle towards another dimension, "for now the / glider vessel of summer / first starship insubstantial as / its voyage enters the wind," brushing the edges of evening, of eternity. But while he is sitting on "The Porch" the Inhabitant listens to sirens "wiring the afternoon — stitching it with steel to the approaching darkness." At the scene of the accident, a child, uninhibited by adult dishonesty, cries, "See his bones!" The poem — which William Meredith called a schizophrenic piece among "flawless poems" — flushes time through the intersection of time's ending for this body "who lay like a sack of winter in the center of a summer street."

The Inhabitant is a sequence of acceptance, finally. Standing in "The Summerhouse" the Inhabitant gazes at his family through the windows, as though he were looking into an aquarium, and accepts the dark imagery of summer, sad, sustaining:

> This is what there is. It is enough: the nightwind, the windows alight in the livingroom, the flowers of the garden touching toward the summerhouse, the neighbors on their porches, the road rolling outward into the darkness under streetlamps moth-haloed and the nighthawk's wing and call.

And he accepts in "The Study" his own alienation from his creativity and self, having merely projected himself into objects, like the lamp, the poem's prime metaphor:

> This is where the Inhabitant lives. These things are his — these books, this music upon which the lamplight falls, upon which he too, once, threw a radiance now eaten by wires tapping the sources of silence and desuetude.

In "The Garden," however, the Inhabitant thrusts against time, using words as runes to spin the world the other way around, back to that primal instant "in that garden / again wearing only these / the tongue's / jewels the ear's / riches eyes like amethyst." This moment of the garden is realized in a different way when the Inhabitant moves into his yard with "the Scythe" "to / whittle / the congregation" of milkweed stalks "into / a large circle then slowly / a smaller one scything / in spirals the / bees moving / always / toward the center." The Inhabitant and his alter-ego, "The crescent blade with its snath / handle," close in with the cutting edge of time towards an ultimate confrontation with the bees. But for once, the Inhabitant controls snaky time and leaves the "bees drinking / one

> nightcap of nectar before dusk cut
> into the still green air

and the Inhabitant leaned
on the snath
against his
blade.

But "The Guestroom" holds the Inhabitant's constant guest, Death, and in the poem the Inhabitant becomes his guest. In "The Basement" — which is a domestication of the legend of Orpheus and Eurydice — there hides a doll for which the Inhabitant's daughter cries. The father finds it, but finds as well his own sense of decay and corrosion poised against the timeless world of the child.

The Inhabitant hears only the keening of silence through time, as he weaves his life in and out of dreams. He dreams of that impossible She in "The Bedroom" — "He was without that dream of absences which grasp and do not grasp, wishless to keep her midnight hues: blue and stone, magnificent, where nothing ever ends." He comes, however, to "the moment of waking, already remembrance," and "Too late he has found it to be one more dream." He rises, remembering sleep and dream on an impossible sea, brooded over by the presence of that she who "clothes the night with a curved phrase."

The critic of *The Inhabitant* can only touch the surface of that which has touched him deeply. The poems pulse with life, reflect the angles of day and night, light linked by the consciousness of a single man, and become an allegory of all solitary inhabitants of the flesh. We, like "The Portrait of a Clown," find our "lips...at the edge of some-thing," always on the brink — of what? Truth? Life? Ourselves? Merely the next moment within our walls?

The house chews at people, drinks time, endures, even as transient inhabitants eat and drink within its living walls. Appropriately, one of the Inhabitant's consistent metaphors is of weaving. The texture of the poems is rich; its effect upon the reader is deeply woven. Like our own experience these poems are threaded of the many moments of time below and beyond the narrow loom of the present.

Conrad Aiken, one of the twentieth century's finest poets, when he read *The Inhabitant* wrote Turco a letter which was used, with Aiken's permission, on the cover of Turco's next book, *Pocoangelini: A Fantography & Other Poems* (1971): "The Inhabitant is the best new poem I've read in something like thirty years — profoundly satisfying to me, speaks my language, such a relief to have WHOLE meaning again, instead of this pitiable dot-and-dash splinter-poetry, or sawdust cornflakes which we usually get." Referring to Turco's earlier *Awaken, Bells Falling* Aiken continued, "And you're all good. You give me courage to read again, and even to believe again in myself. So you see how handsomely I'm in debt. Thank you! You should be, and will be, better *known*." The reason Aiken responded thus is that the door to the poem

> ...once opened
> the visitor must remain in
>
> that place among the
> Inhabitant's couches and
> violets must be that man
>
> in his house cohabiting
> with the dark
> wife her daughter or both."

II

American Still Lifes is divided into three sections: "Twelve Moons," "Still Lifes," and "Autumn's Tales." "Twelve Moons," as one might infer, contains as many poems as moons. "Still Lifes" consists of a prologue, twenty-seven poems, and an epilogue. "Autumn's Tales" is nine poems long. Immediately we perceive the architecture of the collection.

"Twelve Moons" is a guided tour through the months of a northern climate. Our primary focus is on what the Amerindian moon reveals from month to month on the landscape beneath. The poems are woven in a language upon which a human observer does not intrude. Instead, the intensity of observation insists on our response. We are not told what or how to "think" about the poems; we must tell them what they mean. For me, living in a northern climate, they mean the re-creation of my own myth of the seasons, as I observe what the moon shows of a land that deals in extremes. The closest analogues I know in American literature are Henry Adams' wonderful description of New England contrasts at the beginning of *The Education*, and Thoreau's magnificent swing through the seasons in *Walden*. Turco's work is always original, and always aware of its heritage — one reason for the resonance of the poems.

"Twelve Moons" proves a feeling of natural process occurring away from and regardless of "men...in their villages / dreaming themselves awake." The images of the poems are the vesture of archetypes that exist prior to man and may perhaps survive beyond life. The sound of "footsteps in the earth" or the wakening of a boat may disturb the process, but only temporarily, we infer.

Fish, bird, deer are viewed within a precise shading of light or shadow, clearly at times, and at other moments "through a glass darkly." The ideal stance of man towards all of this would seem to be "to climb / under the cloud and bright song." But, at the end, in "Hunting Moon," men wait:

> Snow nearly hard as hail
>   rustles through the bare branches
>   and settles among the leaves
>
> at the roots of the forest.
>   In its den of earth
>   a bear dreams of berries,

of fish gleaming in the shallows.
　　A herd of deer
　　　　shifts edgily in a clearing,

the young bucks shivering.
　　From a distance
　　　　a jay cries

across the gray air.
　　They are in the wood,
　　　　the band of men,

downwind and quiet.
　　The wind begins to rise.
　　　　The snow starts to flake and drift.

Predators enter the woods.　We sense the invasion of man upon the woodlands of life itself.

These poems represent a subtle retelling of "The Fall of Man" played through the prism of twelve separate months. The sequence represents a chronology, a "history," and, perhaps, a negative teleology. If the poems imply the fragility of life, however, we infer the permanency of the nature that underlies its living manifestations.

III

"Still Lifes" seems also to represent a kind of "history," but here the poems are too subtle, too partaking of whatever "art" may be, for the clumsy non-art form known as "literary criticism." My response must be impressionistic, and even more subjective than is most criticism. What I feel, however, is language charged with a repressed consciousness, as if one's unconscious were invited upward to do the "interpreting."

The colonial village over which the articulate and descriptive "camera-eye" begins to rove is deserted, as indeed the "lost" colony of Roanoke was found to be when the British relief expedition at last managed to get through. In fact, the second poem in the sequence, "The Colony," after the prologue, "Landscape," ends with a near-quote from the journal that describes what the would-be rescuers found at Roanoke:

THE COLONY

Rising out of the summer woods
there is a column of smoke
beginning to fade into the sky where,
now and then, a tern or oriole

stitches stillness with a call
and emptiness with a curve of plumage.
The palisade stands open.
The living quarters yawn shadow

into the heat. The fires are cold,
their ash white and fine as snow
on the bare places in the grass.
The blacksmith's tongs lie where they were left;

a water barrel has rolled,
dry as the August wind,
into a corner of the compound.
The woods stand close,

but in them there is no echo —
only the needle rustle of the pines.
Moving inland.
The bark on the log paling

has not begun to show moss,
but one of the chief trees or posts
at the right side of the entrance
has the bark taken off,

and five feet from the ground
in fair capital letters is graven
CROATOAN without any cross
or sign of distress.

What has happened here? Why are the fires cold, the colonial utensils rusting? An Indian raid? The Plague? One gets the eerie feeling that some antique version of the neutron bomb has wafted through this structured but uninhabited "society." An occasional footprint, the impress of hoof and wheel in snowfall as the poems press on through the 17th, the 18th, the 19th centuries, but "If anything moves it is a naked branch," as in "The Maple Works." The poems move, as this one itself says, "out of the unknown toward the forsaken."

We seem to be on Keats' urn, where the little town is emptied, "and not a soul to tell / Why thou art desolate, can e'er return." Nature seems to represent stasis, invisibility, when contrasted with more basic process: "peeling wood / ...musts to lichen near the gate" of "The Tollhouse." "Musts," of course, conveys "necessity" within its duplicity. "The bell rings twice," but we feel its summons as a result of the wind's will, and that the echo melts unheard into twilight. But even the wind is implicit in "The Tollhouse," which ends with a magnificent metaphor. The dark river that cleaves the earth together in daylight, cleaves it asunder at night. Even the villagers who come to "The Mill" "in mufflers and shawls" seem to be "shadow," ghosts of a former time who brood over New England before the camera eye moves south and west over the rest of America. The poems, like "The Stockyard," inhabit "a memory / of slow passage."

And we move on in time as well, to "The Observation Tower" near which there is a car in which "a radio plays the blues," to a world of "streetlamps," a modern church with all the paraphernalia of Sunday-school, "garages...by a gravel drive" belonging to the parsonage beside "The Church," to bathrooms in the houses of the epilogue, "Prothalamion," "where men stand behind glass to gaze into glass, / to feel an edge of steel against hair and flesh."

The mirrors suggest what may be happening — we reflect on the infinite regress implicit in the mirrors and realize, perhaps, that we have found a window into the past. The wraith of former times haunts the present with a way of life, and the lives that followed that way, merely physically erased from the American landscape. The effect of the sequence cannot be described, but I'll make an effort:

As people move into this world of the poem, we recognize, reflexively and reflectively, the presence of people in the earlier poems of the deserted places which suddenly come alive with the activity seemingly suspended in that former time. We recognize, as Hartley says, that "the past is another country — they do things differently there." What we have in "Still Lifes" is, as the final poem says, "a wedding of moss and streets." Whatever seems to be gone continues to lurk above, around, beneath the macadam poured over "deep-down things," as Hopkins calls them. Even more implicit is that modern man and woman could disappear more completely than have the inhabitants of the history that drifts through the present. We recall the "column of smoke" with which the sequence begins at Roanoke.

That I must be impressionistic about the sequence argues Turco's brilliant success. The poems insist on response, even if the response is inadequate. "Poetry," after all, as Frost wisely says, "is what evaporates from all translations." Most modern poetry is delivered already evaporated. But not these poems, this poem, "Still Lifes." I leave it to readers to discern in my response a possible line of approach, but, more important, I leave it to them to develop their response to the suggestive depth and culminating impact of the poems.

121

IV

The last nine poems, "Autumn's Tales," portray a snowstorm approaching a modern town; they are snapshots taken over a few minutes of time, beginning with close-ups of a neighborhood and then trucking back for longer shots, each poem — each "frame" — showing both the landscape and the development of the storm until, in the last wide-angle "Vista" shot, the camera-eye loses sight of the village in the full fury of a blizzard and the falling night.

"The Neighborhood," with its repetition of "settle" and its variants, has the effect of a sestina. That effect asserts a powerful gravitational pull to the poem's "meaning" down into its fine ironies. As "free" as the poem may seem to be, it works precisely because Turco knows the form underlying what the poem "says," the form that releases the poem into its feeling of "freedom." The final two stanzas of "The Trees" create a wonderfully complex metaphor that makes of the sky at once an ocean and a ship, and of a kite an emblem of the earth's slow-roll into darkness:

> A kite, worn thin by scraping
> against the sky, rustles
> along the prow of night:
>
> It is a figurehead of tissue,
> of soft wood, its ragged tail
> caught in shadow, pulling darkness.

While the craftsmanship is magnificent, it is the servant of a transcendent effect.

At the end of "The Street" (as it were), "the curbs of vision" pick up the specificity of street per se and suggest the limitations on our ability to see anything beyond what we can see from our defined perspective. A neat duplicity of language, itself seemingly a limited quantity until Turco gets hold of it, suggests limitations, both physical and emotional.

"The Fences" become at once snow-laden walls and a force that "will cut through dusk / as though they were knives with white edges." The magic that metaphor is created for dazzles us with its sleight-of-word. And at the end — a reminder of Wordsworth's "The Prelude," as "The hills rise over the valley, / and the river is lost." Twilight moves in finally, as it has encroached all along, to give this book an ending as effective and as "realized" as is the last page of a fine novel.

V

The setting for the poems in *The Green Maces of Autumn, Voices in an Old Maine House* (2002) is Blinn's Hill, Dresden, Maine, its houses, barns and gravestones, beginning in the middle of the eighteenth century and coming up to the present. Each poem except for the first, "Albums," is a dramatic monologue spoken by a person whose name is the title of the poem — "Jessie Baker," "Jean Court," "Ruth Carr," "Ann Pullen," and so forth. This book is about haunting and the haunted, not in any melodramatic way, but as the tick of the clock is repeated in the click of the bone, and as people absorb what goes on around them and incorporate the outside world into their unique perceptions and misprisions.

We get, as we expect from Turco, that concentration on the almost unnoticed detail and the concatenation of tiny instants into fragmentary wholeness — or absence, as in the deafness of "Amanda Pullen," for whom "stillness is crystalline." She wonders how long it has been "Since there was a touch, or a / taste, even of smoke, in this white air." The people who "live" within the walls have time to contemplate what is not there. "Timothy Bourne" has no child to "heft," no way of "feeling the weight of the future." His wife, "Margaret Bourne," feels the "vagrant weightlessness of shadow / or breeze, its motion...silent / as evening fading among silhouettes." For "Randall Bourne" the past becomes his remembered hope for the future: "Those were the summers of events hanging / in the imagination like thunderheads / glimpsed through the attic window...."

What is not there becomes what is there. "Harriet Bourne" remembers the sacrament of an August clambake in steaming, shell-strewn detail. Or does she? "Perhaps the happy voices were / echoes in the walls, and the faces figments of my contemplation, a twist / of the eyes in the blank room of summer." Awaiting spring, "Bertha Bourne" hears, "now and again, rumors / of resurrection," but her husband "is gone...his body is divorced from mine, his voice / an echo from frozen springs."

On the hillside above the house lies the graveyard, and it has substance amid the echoes: "I shall turn / gray as the lichen," says "John Pullen Bourne," "on the stone / that weights my body beneath the winter day." The headstones stare down upon the farmhouse. Women disappear among the memorials and then return, "their hands empty of stalk and blossom, / for they had left them with the one / who had left them".

These poems are splendidly crafted quantitative syllabics, subtly rhythmic in ways that "free verse" can never be. They insist that we listen and look and respond to the unique voice of each speaker. Emerging from the rhythmic structure of these poems are those language tricks that Turco, the verbal magician, performs for us. "Julia Pullen," dead these twenty-five years, talks of "The dark, as some child slides / my drawer to now" — a homely simile that powerfully clenches the inevitable to the familiar. "My sister," says "Margaret Pullen," "moves now like the ghost of a gown filled with winds." "Jessie Baker," driving home, listens to the "small talk of tappets and valves" under the hood of her blue Buick. They say "nothing / of cells raging like wild worms through the host / of themselves," for flesh must perforce be hospitable to the cancer consuming it. Grandfather Pullen, unwinding string from a kite lifting from the top of the hill is nevertheless "caught in the scrimmage of children."

Any good poet plays with language. The question is always at which level the game is played, as in "Philip Bourne":

> Like a friar asking alms, the chickadee
> proffered its black cap at the windowpane
> where the bankrupt feeder wove
> in the wind.

Here observation is not, I think, overweighed by metaphor. Whether that is the case with this passage from "Herbert Torrey" I leave to the reader, as Dr. Johnson left Donne's "Valediction":

> That fourth of July a sly laugh
> dogged our fancy. Uncle John,
> the old wag, taled off again.

Like *The Sketches, Pocoangelini, The Inhabitant,* and *American Still Lifes,* Turco's poetic sequence *The Green Maces of Autumn* tells a story, and, again like the earlier series, the narrative linkages are suppressed, leaving the fragments to suggest much more than they contain individually. The names in the "Albums" are gone: "Whose child is this that sits / in the dusty shadows — whose dust, whose shade?" The child is an anonymous ghost because Jessie Baker forgot to put "names / against heydays." Even the names on the gravestones in the cemetery are "eroded by rains / etched in lichen, / ...obscured by herbs and seasons." The names themselves deafen, become senile and arthritic, or as Turco puts it in a superb synesthesia that attributes the process of forgetting to the dead, "The dates are sometimes hard of recollection." Nor will they ever be collected again, these "great spirals of the past falling, / moments coming to rest."

The success of a magician's sleight-of-hand insists upon our willingness to suspend our disbelief. Magic depends on us. And so it is with this sequence of poems. The "much more" trembles in-around-behind the houses, barns, and stones of Blinn's Hill. The poems pull from us echoings of our own past. The images catch us at our memories and touch the years when we played catch with Dad or held our infants in our arms. Those moments do not come again. Since an echo is a resonating circle, the poems touch what is to come, when our own smiles will be faded and beaming under the splintered plastic of the album.

Much of Turco's work, like that of his older contemporary craftsmen (Louis Coxe, Richard Eberhart, and Howard Nemerov spring to mind) will find its way into whatever future lies before us. The qualities that tend to make Turco's work "too good" for contemporary celebrity will earn him several precious pages in anthologies yet unborn. The sensitive reader, however, educated to what poetry is and is not, should be reading him now. Turco will reward that experience, as the reader finds his perceptions honed, his imagination challenged, and his awareness of language, world, and life are immeasurably enhanced.

TERRA IMAGINARIA
by Gene Van Troyer

I

LEWIS TURCO'S *POETRY: AN INTRODUCTION THROUGH WRITING* is one book I wish I had discovered way back when I was an undergraduate student, for it would have cured me of a malady all too common among beginning writers and poets, and kept a lot of egg off my face as a result. That malady is this: Beginners confuse form with tradition. As Turco takes pains to point out in the introduction to this text, form and tradition are two very different things. Tradition is the way a particular form has primarily been used, but the form in itself is independent of tradition.

As should be obvious to anyone, all poems have form or structure, regardless of whether the poet is inventing his own or employing a well-established formal structure such as the triolet, the sonnet, or the haiku — as Turco did in *Seasons of the Blood*. While each of these have their own specific formal requirements, it is not necessary to pay heed to the traditions which surround them in order to use them well. Finely tuned thought and feeling, and not tradition, is the game. Fifteen years ago, when I first began to experiment with poetry, I was unaware of this. Such guided instruction as this book offers could have saved me nearly a decade's worth of hard knocks.

What this text offers is an introduction to scores upon scores of different forms and modes of writing poetry through actually writing them. As it is an instructional text, each section is concluded with a series of exercises intended to teach the reader or student the functions of various structures through actual writing practice. From a technical viewpoint it covers verse and prose modes and prosodies, spatial prosody, poetic levels, sonics, tropes, schemas, the major genres — lyric, narrative, and dramatic poetry, and the minor genres — didactic, occasional, bucolic, confessional, and satiric poetry. Just about everything. The only thing left out is the view of poetry that has come out of applied linguistics, and which is alternately known as linguistic criticism or stylistics — but *Poetry: An Introduction* predates this recent view by about four years.

Turco is careful to note that his book is not intended as a "creative writing" text, but merely to introduce students to the complexities and densities of poetry and poetic diction. In spite of this overly timid caution, I think it would make an excellent addition to any writer's basic reference shelf as a guide to form and technique; and there is much in it that could easily be adapted to creative writing courses.

My only objections to this text involve certain matters of terminology. For instance, the text refers to "long vowels" and "short vowels." There is no such thing in English as vowels that are "long" or "short." In the linguistic sense (and as anyone who has studied syllabic languages knows), lengthening a vowel sound radically changes the meaning of a word. The fact of the absence of long or short vowels in English is amply demonstrated by any English speaker who is learning Japanese. I can't count the number of times that I said "beauty parlor" when I meant to say "hospital" because I said *liyooin* instead of *lyooin*, or "Japanese street" when I meant "bird" because I had uttered *toori* instead of *tori*. In the English language one can say "help" or "heeelp" and the basic meaning does not change, though the emphasis does ("need" to "dire need"). As a matter of fact, one can even change radically some vowel sounds in English without messing up the meaning, as in "Ahm gohn ohvah theah" for "I'm going over there." Anyway, we have "high" and "low" vowels in English, but not long and short — unless of course one is speaking about emphatics. Lengthened vowels in English have a powerful effect on nuance and connotation because they change the stress placed on a word, and in this context "long" or "short vowel" makes sense.

I digress. This book has long been out of print, but if one can't find it, then a copy of Turco's, *The New Book of Forms: A Handbook of Poetics* (1986) is surely available and it is a combination of his 1968 *The Book of Forms* and *Poetry: An Introduction Through Writing.* James Dickey says on the cover of the paperback edition of *The New Book* that it "Belongs in the hands of every poet, student, and teacher, for the greater good of the art."

II

Imaginary bestiaries are not uncommon, and have roots which extend back over the millennia to the great zoological texts compiled by the Greeks and Chinese, wherein such fabulous creatures as the griffin, the phoenix, the chimera, the tapir, and the sphinx were to be found soberly discussed side-by-side with such mundane creatures as dogs, chickens, cats and bears. As knowledge of the world grew, however, and investigators failed to locate any physical evidence of the more fabulous animal life in their copious texts, such creatures fell prey to the editor's pen — a kind of extinction all its own, and a curious inversion of that old dictum about the pen being mightier than the sword.

Many are the species long thought to be extinct, however, which have actually found obscure ecological niches in which to thrive. Imaginary beasts are no exception. Their niche, like the bolt-holes of certain former "facts" of bygone days, became legend, myth, poetry — the stuff of the human imagination, which is ever on the lookout for a decent symbol. It is only natural that great zoological texts should therefore have been compiled to detail the various flora and fauna of terra imaginaria. Two famous Renaissance examples were published by Edward Topsell, *The History of Four-Footed Beasts* (1607) and *The History of Serpents* (1608), which reappeared recently as Topsell's *Histories of Beasts* edited by Malcolm South in 1981. Another is *A Medieval Bestiary*, translated and introduced by T. J. Elliott, with wood engravings by Gillian Tyler (1971), though both of these are prose, not verse. John Ciardi's *An Alphabestiary* (1967) is the more likely inspiration here.

Most bestiaries treat their fabulous subjects as if they were beings independent of the human imagination, which is perfectly valid and in the tradition of asking, "What if...?" Even Borges does this to some extent, though he probes more deeply into the mythic, archetypal nature of imaginary beings, seating them more centrally in the psychological continuum of the human consciousness.

In *A Cage of Creatures* (1978) and its companion *A Maze of Monsters* (1986), Lewis Turco takes his creatures several steps deeper into the psychological continuum, locating them in their actual residence, the imagination. His primary focus in the first volume is on people, and those traits which they have in common with the imaginary beings of the title. In this chapbook Turco presents us with nine poems: "Dybbuk," "Nasnas," "Sasquatch" (dedicated to John Ciardi), "Yeti," "Homunculus," "Zombie," "Grendel," "Golem," and "Fetch." In the second collection there are seventeen poems, "A-Bao-A-Qu," "Basilisk and Cockatrice," "Chimera," "Ent," "Imago," "Juggernaut," "Kraken" (originally published in *The Weed Garden* as "The Voyagers"), "Leviathan," "Minotaur," "Odradek," "Phoenix and Salamander," "Querule," "Roc," "Uroboros" (which was "The Worm" in *The Weed Garden*), "Vielfras," "Werewind," and "Xoanon."

In the "Foreword" to the larger chapbook Turco writes, "The major source for *A Maze of Monsters* is Jorge Luis Borges' *The Book of Imaginary Beings*, though other sources have also been used." And he continues a bit farther on, "These poems are approximately half of an unpublished manuscript alphabestiary of fantastic beings titled *The Book of Beasts*. The first half, consisting of only the humanoid monsters of the manuscript, was published as *A Cage of Creatures*...." Their reflection-as-reality in the human countenance begins immediately with "Dybbuk".

Not all of the metaphors are as directly stated as this, but something of the human is to be found in all of these creatures: how else is a fabulous creature to be described realistically, if not in terms emotionally understandable to a human being? Of course, once a monster is put into human terms, it becomes disturbingly human-like, as in

FETCH

To step out of a bedroom
into a forest of darkness;
to find oneself naked among brambles
and shagbark, a low wind making the flesh rise.
To turn and discover there is no door,
only bellbloom and shadow.

And this is waking, the path
beaten hard beneath heaven, stars
among limbs bare of season. And between
trees, glass — dark sheets parsing silence without
image. In the wood only the mutter
and crool of water wending.

Pause and touch: Merely surface
smooth and cold among the boles. Search:
Only the ghost of reflection paling
under gaze. Walk, cover the ground. Know there is
neither graith nor tackle to take the wood.
Move as through one more tunnel.

Stop when you feel him near. Strain
to see who stands in the way, who
holds out his hand, loof and hardel: It is
another mirror of the wood — no: Likeness
of quicksilver. Behind him, a bedroom
lies rumpled in a gilt frame.

It is dark, but he is known.
He is the beast of whom they have
spoken so often in living rooms and
dreams. It is a familiar forest. This is
one's own path. It is the Fetch beckoning
welcome to the crystal glade.

While the subjects of all of these poems are monsters, the tone is of fantasy rather than the creepy-crawlies of horror poetry (or, as is all too often the case, the turbid dumbling of a disagreeably bad dream that a great deal of horror poetry ends up conveying). If humans have a human condition, then surely monsters have a monster condition, and Turco describes it — feelingly, and at times with a wry, bemused humor, as in this poem from *Maze*:

ODRADEK

At first one might take it
merely for another mathom:
a useless treasure such as may be found
in a littered attic or lost
within a dim closet, toward the back —

star-shaped, made of sticks, wrapped
in thread-ends, knotted and tangled,
of many textures, thicknesses, colors.
There is a small crossbar of wood
glued by an end to the star's center, and

held to the rod, at right
angles, another rod — a leg
on which, together with a starpoint, it
stands upright. If you address it
on the stairs where often it lurks, it will

tell its name, the tattered
threads trembling, and then laugh like dry
leaves rustling. Look for Odradek and it
   will be absent for as long as
you remember. But in the fall, perhaps,

a solemn wind wrapping
   the eaves, you will climb dusty stairs
into the garret, looking for — you know
   not what: A sheet of paper, sere
at the edges, on which your father wrote;

   a clock with a painted
   face, time run out of it. And there,
behind a chest, near the dry carcass of
   a moth, a fly, Odradek will
stand raveling. You will ask, "Where have you

   been?" But it will stand mute,
   spindling silence, draggling shadow.
You will shrug at last in the chill, droning
   afternoon, begin to rummage.
When you look up, Odradek will have gone.

There is something else going on in these poems that is worthy of
mention. Poetry is sometimes characterized as the means by which the
absolute limits of language are tested, and the agency through which
new modes of expression are discovered. I believe it was W. H. Auden
who once observed that one means of accomplishing this was through
the resurrection of archaic words long fallen from usage, and long since
edited from our dictionaries, if indeed they ever made it into the
dictionaries in the first place — a fate not unlike that which befell the
fabulous creatures mentioned at the outset of this review. Turco has set

himself the task of resurrecting some of these words, and writes in the forewords to both chapbooks that "The archaic words used in the poems are from Charles MacKay's *The Lost Beauties of the English Language*, originally published in 1874 and reprinted...in 1969. The author agrees with Mr. MacKay that there are many words that ought to be restored to English, and this is a small attempt to reinstate a few of them. One hopes that the contexts in which the words appear will suggest their definitions to the extent that a glossary is unnecessary." The results are colorful and playful, and already such words as dumble, skime, clointer, crambles, chirming and roaky have been added to my vocabulary. For these words alone *A Cage of Creatures* and *A Maze of Monsters* are more than worth the low price of admission.

What's that you say? What do these words mean? Well, buy the books! After all, language comes alive in poetry, doesn't it?

III

While not exactly speculative poetry, much which a third chapbook — *Seasons of the Blood* (1980) — contains is most certainly well within the fantasy vein, and makes it into science fiction at least once. The subject matter is straight out of *Tarot*, with the majority of the poems titled after suits and Arcana, and various individual cards (i.e. "The Hanged Man," "Death," "The Hermit," "The Tower"). The poems are all cast in various of the Japanese forms: mondo, katauta, sedoka, choka, tanka, somonka, waka, haiku, and senryu. The poet executes these forms with a deft hand, though Western symbolism sits uneasily in Asian poetic forms which eschew the sort of thing Turco is doing — but then, he has made them into Western forms, and they do work. Here is

CUPS

Moon takes the tide where
a tide must go: Light pierces
the hardest crystal.

These poems are written in the form of dialogues, as of one seeking and being given advice by a card reader. It lends them the power that such consultative procedures can often have, as in "Correspondence," which returns to the subject of "Uroboros" from *Maze*:

CORRESPONDENCE

There is a black hole
in space, where the universe
is disappearing.
This is what I have read.
The scientists frighten me.

Have you never heard
of the hermetic dragon?
Do not be afraid.
What disappears is not lost.
The snake is eating its tail.

Stylistically, the poems are impeccable. If they come across as cryptic, it is because they are intended to function as Oracles: not as mirrors of the truth, but as tools through which an understanding of the truth may be approached. They collaborate with the reader, rather than instruct. Let me close with

PENTACLES

The heart is a coin
of fire. How shall we spend it?
How is the sun spent?

THE ANACHRONIST
by Gerhard Zeller

IN AN ESSAY ON LEWIS TURCO in *The Encyclopedia of American Literature* (Continuum, 1998), R. S. Gwynn has written, *"The Book of Forms* (1968) and its successor *The New Book of Forms* (1986) have now influenced two generations of students and poets, most prominently the group known as The New Formalists (a term Turco anticipated when he began to write approvingly of 'neo-formalism' in the early 1980's)." A bit later in his article Gwynn writes, "For a number of years Turco has employed an alter-ego, one Wesli Court (an anagram of his name), to construct light verse and formal tours de force, including many of the sample poems in *The New Book of Forms."*

This interview was conducted on July 4th, 1980, in Dresden, Maine, where Wesli Court was the proprietor of the Mathom Bookshop and Bindery. It was accepted for publication by *Modern Poetry Studies*, but that periodical suspended publication before "The Anachronist" appeared, and the interview was not published until 1998. Gerhard Zeller was for more than three decades a member of the English faculty of the State University of New York College at Oswego. He died in the summer of 1996. Wesli Court still "lives" in Dresden where he helps Lewis Turco run his antiquarian bookshop.

Gerhard Zeller. From the scant biographical information I've been able to gather, I understand that you are largely self-educated. You've spent most of your time working on the Great Lakes, and what interests me most recently in my reading through your first book, *Courses in Lambents* [Oswego: Mathom, 1977], is your constant reference to out-of-the-way poets. The longest poem in your book is "Robyn and Makyn" which you say is "out of the Scots of Robert Henryson." I'm curious to know where you picked up your interest in these virtually forgotten poets of the past. For example, who is Henryson?

Wesli Court. Henryson was a Scottish poet who lived in the period just after Chaucer and who wrote in the dialect called Scots, which is still very close to Middle English. I became interested in these old poets because I'm interested in traditional lyric poetry, and I write in nothing but traditional lyric forms, although I'm not above an occasional experiment in meters and rhymes. It seems to me that some of the most interesting poetry in English is lyric poetry, and that some of the most interesting poems are quite ancient.

Zeller. It seems to me you are resuscitating ancient forms, not just the poems of old poets like Henryson. You seem in all of your published poems, including *Curses and Laments* [Stevens Point: *Song*, No. 5, 1978], to show an interest in forms that aren't being used by other poets, such as the Welsh forms and Anglo-Saxon alliterative measures. Don't you think this makes you something of a modern anachronism?

Court. It's true that I'm a literary anachronist. However, Lewis Turco needs examples of many of these ancient verse patterns for his revision of *The Book of Forms*, and he has asked me to help him out with modern versions of medieval poems in the bardic forms.

Zeller. What do you think you accomplish by going back to these forms that are so much out of the mainstream? How does it feel to be moving constantly against the grain?

Court. Well, I don't think of it that way. I consider it as merely going back to the roots of English poetry. I should have said "British" poetry, because I'm interested in the Welsh and Gaelic forms as well. Although there's a great deal of what passes for poetry being written today, it's boring, most of it. I think the most interesting poems of the twentieth century very often were lyric poems, such as those by the early Ezra Pound, e.e. cummings, Edwin Arlington Robinson, Robert Frost, William Butler Yeats, Wallace Stevens — these poets have been credited with having given American twentieth-century poetry new directions which have been picked up, supposedly, by poets writing since the 1950s, but in fact many of them were really excellent traditional metrical poets, and many of the greatest poems of this century are metrical. Not many people think of it in these terms, but it's a fact.

I can think of other poets, for instance Vachel Lindsay, who was a so-called "modernist," who was a lyric poet; John Crowe Ransom and, a little later, Theodore Roethke, who were wonderful lyric poets writing in the prosody called podics, or "folk meters," which was the system used in the old Scottish border ballads of the fifteenth century, of many of the poems of the early Renaissance poet John Skelton, and the nursery rhymes of the seventeenth century. When people think of twentieth-century poetry they think of poems written by people such as T. S. Eliot, but even he was writing in metrical verse very often — *Old Possum's Book of Practical Cats* is the most obvious example — so I think that the direction of most recent poetry is misguided. I think that a poet ought to be interested in the sonic level, at the very least, and the thing that interests most readers is sound and rhythm, good imagery, and those are the things I'm still interested in also.

To say that I'm a throwback misses the point. What I am is in the mainstream, and all these other people are going off on tangents. I suspect that within the next hundred years, perhaps sooner, we're going to see a return to this mainstream of lyric poetry writing. Therefore, I will be considered by the folk of the future to have been in the avant garde.

Zeller. Well, you've probably answered my question already, but in one of the poems in *Courses in Lambents* — why did you give your first two books such similar titles? — you have a character named Ollie. Would you read it?

Court. Certainly.

SEPTEMBER PLAY SONG

Red Rover, Red Rover,
Let Alice come over,
For Alice is a scary girl
Whose hair is wild, whose curls are gold,
As bold as lightning by the river
Moving bluely to the sea.

Red Rover, Red Rover,
Let Billy come over —
Billy wicked, Billy bad,
Billy crazy as the daisies
In the pastures blooming mad
Among the grasses.

Red Rover, Red Rover,
Let Ollie come over.
Let sad little Ollie who loved pretty Polly,
Who lost fickle Polly to raindrops and time,
Let Ollie come over
All mossy with rime.

Red Rover, Red Rover,
Let Whozis come over.
For Whozis is looking for Alice and Bill,
For Ollie and Poll lying cold in the clover....
Red Rover, Red Rover,
Push all of them over.

Zeller. The effect of that poem is chilling, but Ollie is, you say, "all mossy with rime." You wouldn't see that as a self-criticism — being mossy?

Court. I'd consider it a compliment.

Zeller. You've given quite a pastiche of literary figures that you feel akin to, writers as diverse as Pound and Eliot on the one hand and, on the other, Vachel Lindsay, but all of these poets, with the exception of Lindsay, were noted for their intellectual avant-gardism based on strong academic credentials. You, on the other hand, have no such background. It's as though you are a throwback to those nineteenth century Romantic poets who were essentially uneducated or self-educated.

Court. It is absolutely true that I taught myself, afloat and ashore, all these traditional techniques I continue to use. No teacher taught them to me. But on the other hand, what academic background did Frost have? And he is one of the century's most formal poets. Many poets traditionally have been self-educated in versewriting. In fact, before the 1940's and the rise of the college "writing workshops," which are a phenomenon of the postwar period, nearly all poets have been self-educated in poetry composition. Hart Crane is another obvious example.

Zeller. The one thing that I think differentiates you from most of the poets we've mentioned, at least in the bulk of their work, is a sense of humor, frequently bawdy, that runs through much of your work. This morning as I reread *Courses in Lambents* I noted that in your opening "Proem: The Muses' Ball" you say that the test of a poet is that "the verses jest solemnly." Would you read that poem so that we can talk about it?

Court. I'd be happy to do so:

PROEM: THE MUSES' BALL

A Dialogue of Sonnets

Narcissus. I've had it, on good authority, that the best
poems are those which are delimited
and which, within strict bounds, are amply fed
on wit and learning. There is but one test
one need apply: does the verser jest
solemnly? Which was the sage who said,
"A solitary talent, well directed,
shall make a man the Muse's welcome guest?

I can't abide that deadly social trance.
I shall bed down with every busty rime
that bends to dalliance. There is no time
for proper posing if the pen would dance —
go sit and sip with Miss Calliope.
Erato is no hostess. She's a she.

Endymion. Discourse is social too. If you must dance,
go reel Virginia in, rhumba, cakewalk —
but some of us would rather sit and talk.
We do it quietly — by choice, not chance.
Still others of us will not join the fun
because our plainer muses do not shine
like public chandeliers. The finest wine
comes by the goblet, never by the tun.
We have our place in this, the Muses' Ball,
as you have yours. There's room enough and more
for you and your coy mistress on the floor;
must you usurp Euterpe's bit of wall?

Leave us to muse here while you step and roar.
It is too easy to seduce a whore.

Narcissus. Okay, I will.

Zeller. Which of those two poets is you?

Court. Both.

Zeller. Do you believe yourself to jest solemnly in most of your poems?

Court. Yes. I think that life is a tragicomedy. If a poet is going to be a whole poet he has to take into account both the solemn and the joyous, both the hysterically funny and the despairing. If I am going to reflect human nature, I must write of both. Poetry is simultaneously a game and a deadly serious contest. Life is a serious game.

Zeller. In that same poem you quote an unnamed sage as saying, "A solitary talent, well directed / shall make a man the muse's welcome guest." Even if your publication record isn't vast, do you consider yourself to be such a guest? And who is the sage?

Court. I am, just as I am both poets. You have to remember the subtitle of the poem; it's a debate between two kinds of poets, between "Narcissus" and "Endymion." The former is a romantic extrovert, and the latter is a classic introvert. While I probably have both elements within me, I tend to side with the quieter Endymion.

Zeller. You seem to have not just a split personality, but a shattered one — how many of you are there? Isn't "Wesli Court" just a pen-name?

Court. All my names are "pen names." I once did an interview with two of my other selves ["Interview with a Split Personality," *New England Review*, i:5, April-May 1970]. I also have a personal muse, whose name is Jascha — he's a gargoyle, and he sits on my right shoulder. If I'm not his welcome guest, at least he is mine.

Zeller. Let's talk about the bawdy side. You seem to have, especially in your second book, *Curses and Laments* — which appears to be at least an echo of your first book of poems — a great number of downright lewd poems. How much of a part does sexuality play in your work?

Court. Again, that's an element of human nature that hasn't been treated with great candor by contemporary poets. Not to say that there aren't dirty poems around, but the bawdy has been neglected. In the preface to *Curses and Laments* I say, "What's wrong with a curse? Red Hanrahan wrote a great curse against age which Yeats recorded, but the genre has been much neglected since then. A curse ought to be intemperate. A curse ought not to be cursory, nor ought it to be over-inflated. It ought to last as long as it takes to take effect on its object; it ought to be well-tempered, and there should be nothing of the reflective about it at all." Would you like a sample?

Zeller. Of course.

Court. This poem was supposed to be written in the French form called the virelai, but it refused to fit and would only manifest itself as an acrostic rondeau. All I could do was pun on the word "virelai," in an anagram which begins the poem:

VIRELAI AVORTÉE EN FORME
DE RONDEAU ACROSTICHE
Anagram: "Ring a Virile Lady."

V irelai, won't you come? Just so,
I t will have to be the rondeau
R ising to love. Nor will you spurt,
G alloping response to the quirt
I n my hand. You will merely go
N ag on me, like that bland "No!"
I n my lady's lips. You will grow
A trifle testy if I flirt.

L ai, won't you?
R ing a virile lady and blow
A s you will, winding to and fro,
D iking up happiness and hurt.
L eman, once more before I squirt,
E asing off this sheet...yes, I know:
Y ou won't lai.

Don't you feel that it's about time that all the feelings we have, including hatred, ought to be put into words again?

Zeller. Most certainly. There seems, however, to be, both in the serio-comic verses and in the bawdy poems that occur in your work, a strong undertone of darkness, death, and despair. Earlier this morning I was reading in your manuscripts an unpublished poem titled "Reflections in an Attic Room" [since published in Miller Williams' *Patterns of Poetry*, Louisiana State University, 1986], which, as is so common with your work, is couched in an ancient form, the sonnet redoublé. In the poem, you speak of "A skeleton of what is my concern: / The meaning of it all." And, in reference to that a bit earlier in the poem you say, "...we merely lie / Noting nothings echoing." Is that your vision of life?

Court. Being alive is a very depressing occupation, and, as I said, if I'm going to reflect human nature in all its moods and aspects, I'm going to have to show the dark as well as the light side. I really do live in an attic room. I am perhaps the only poet you'll ever meet who actually lives in a garret, and it gets depressing in my garret where I'm surrounded by the books of these gone, dead poets. You noticed earlier that I'm interested in ancient poems; well, I get to looking, sometimes, at the spines of all these books on my shelves, and I get to thinking about the futility of writing.

There are many poems in many of these books that are simply beautiful, and nobody ever reads them except people like me, and I get

146

to thinking about the people who have written them, how long they've been gone, and then I begin to move forward in time to the point were I, too, am one of those spines standing on a shelf, and I become depressed, and I write about that melancholy.

Zeller. One of your books is dedicated to Ezra Pound, isn't it?

Court. Not a book, a manuscript still unpublished titled, at the moment, *Ancient Music* after a Pound poem which is a modern imitation of the medieval poem that begins, "Sumer is icummen in." A portion of the manuscript will be published soon as a chapbook special issue of Temple University's *Poetry Newsletter*. Its title will be *The Airs of Wales* [Philadelphia, 1981], and it's just the Welsh poems in a collection of modern versions of medieval Welsh, Irish, Scots, Anglo-Saxon and Middle English poems. One of the latter appears in *Curses and Laments*. "The Blacksmiths," a curse from the anonymous Middle English, is, like *Piers Plowman* and *Gawain and the Green Knight*, a late example of Anglo-Saxon alliterative verse. X. J. Kennedy is going to anthologize this poem in his *Tygers of Wrath* [University of Georgia, 1981; reprinted in *World Poetry: An Anthology of Verse from Antiquity to Our Time*, edited by Katharine Washburn and John S. Major, New York: W. W. Norton, 1998]:

THE BLACKSMITHS

Sooty, swart smiths,   Smattered with smoke,
Drive me to death   With the din of their dents.
Such noise at night   No men heard, never!
What knavish cries   And clattering of knocks!
The crooked cretins   Call out, "Coal, coal!"
And blow their bellows   Till their brains burst:
"Huff, puff!" says that one;   "Haff, paff!" that other.
They spit and sprawl   And spill many spells;

147

They gnaw and gnash,   They groan together
And hold their heat   With their hard hammers.
Of bullhide are made   Their broad aprons;
Their shanks be shackled   For the fiery flinders;
They've heavy hammers   That are hard-hafted,
Stark strokes   On a steely stump:
LUS, BUS! LAS, DAS!   Rants the row —
So doleful a dream,   The devil destroy it!
The master lengthens little   And labors less,
Twines a two   And touches a trey:
Tick, tack! hick, hack!   Ticket, tacket! tyke, take!
LUS, BUS! LAS, DAS! Such lives they lead,
These cobblemares: Christ give them grief!
May none of these waterburners   By night have his rest!

Zeller. That's a very Poundian poem in several ways, it seems to me. Pound once spoke of artists being the antennae of the race, and yet in his attempts to put out feelers to the new he was constantly going back to ancient poets in a great number of languages, much in the way that you do, too. Do you feel a kinship with Pound in this habit?

Court. Yes. One of the things that I'm trying to do in these modern versions is breathe new life into the poems of those old masters. The only reason many of them aren't read is because they're written in dialects or languages that are no longer spoken. What I'd like to do is bring back something of the aura and ambience of those poets and their times so that modern readers can enjoy them. Of course, Pound was much interested in similar things throughout his career.

Zeller. Yet, at the time Pound was, and perhaps is still accused today, of being archaic and of trying to dig up forms that cannot really be resurrected and used with effect in the twentieth century. And now that another half-century has passed since Pound engaged in this literary grave-raiding and his message evidently didn't get through, do you feel that this is a profitable line to follow, or do you think that, now we are well into the last quarter of our century, there is a gradual awakening to the kinds of concerns that Pound urged upon young writers?

Court. What do you mean his message didn't get through? It got through to me! I feel that pronouncements to the effect that forms cannot be reused by later generations is just stupid. A form is an abstract pattern, and if someone comes along who has the talent to take that pattern and make a modern, enjoyable poem of it again, as Yeats did and others I've already mentioned, then the stupidity of the statement is made manifest. Still, people say these things. However, I've noticed that such statements are made generally by people who can't do, or haven't tried to do, the hard thing. I've only been publishing these poems for three or four years, but oddly enough, during that time, in this latter-day of "free verse" prose poems, I've had considerable success in the little magazines and in some anthologies, too.

I think people really want to hear the kind of poems Pound was interested in early in his career, and that I am interested in now. I think that there is a rebirth of interest beginning in formal lyric poetry, and that the interest is getting stronger. I believe we have passed through an age of dullness, and now both readers and writers want to try to get some of the primal interest of poetry — that is, in the sounds of the language and in the imagery — back into circulation.

Zeller. Pound was accused by many people of being a poetic charlatan. I know that this charge has been leveled against you as well. In your poem "Terzanelle" from *Courses in Lambents* you say, "The wind's a huckster whose breath blows / Tongues and voices, voices and tongues / Out of a sack of echoes." Are you a huckster, a poetic charlatan?

Court. Well, an artist is a masker, isn't he? We needn't go through all that business that Eliot and the New Critics went through when they talked about the mask, the persona of the poet. Here's what I think about critics anyway — it's a curse from *Curses and Laments*:

ACADEMIC CURSE: AN EPITAPH

Curse him who digs in yellow leaves
　To scrape my twisted tongue
Of twisted songs that once I sang
　Out of a twisted lung!

Rot take the worm that bites my dust.
　May his bowels wither!
I shall make him eat his words
　When he grovels hither.

Writing poetry is telling lies in order to tell the truth, adopting masks in order to merge oneself with a personality that is perhaps alien to one's ordinary nature. Yes, indeed, I am a fraud through and through, but I tell the truth.

THE MIRROR IMAGE:
A RETROSPECTIVE VIEW OF LEWIS TURCO
De Villo Sloan

LEWIS TURCO'S *THE SHIFTING WEB: NEW AND SELECTED POEMS* (1989) is a much-needed retrospective from a significant poet whose work spans three decades. In recent years Turco has become better-known as a proponent of the New Formalism (*The New Book of Forms: A Handbook of Poetics* [1986], *Visions and Revisions of American Poetry* [1986], *The Public Poet* [1991]) than as a skilled poet whose work transcends fashion. The formally varied and philosophically complex verse in this volume sets the record straight.

The first of the book's six sections is problematic. Early work, including a liberal sampling from *Awaken, Bells Falling* (Poems 1959-1967) reveals a precocious but undeveloped talent. These poems bring to mind Pound's famous comment about the "stale cream puffs" of his early career; however, the inclusion of these pieces is necessary when one places them in the context of the thematic structure of the book.

In an early poem such as "The Forest Beyond the Glass" the reader finds the images of the house and its environs that span all of Turco's work (*Awaken* 28-29; *Shifting Web* 20-21). Everywhere in these early poems a keen, observing eye is evident. "An Ordinary Evening is Cleveland" is a longer lyric that establishes a consistent tone and explores the boundaries of language: "The street has a black tongue: do you / hear him, Mistress Alley, wooing / you with stones?" (*Awaken* 20-23, *Shifting Web* 15-17). In these poems Turco begins the long process of transforming the ordinary things of the world into the extraordinary world of his poems.

At the beginning of *The Shifting Web* the poems are preoccupied with the inherent duality of the western tradition. This can be interpreted in a number of ways. One reader might say Turco's main theme is an exploration of the relationship between the mind and the body; another might say self and other; and a postmodern might point to the relationship between the signifier and the signified. In understanding Turco's work, however, interpretation is less important than process. Let it suffice to say that the work is largely preoccupied with the apparently irreconcilable nature of oppositions, and its rich ambiguity offers many possibilities for specific interpretations.

The book's second section includes poems from *Pocoangelini: A Fantography and Other Poems* (1971) and *The Inhabitant* (1970), two of his most ambitious cycles, and also the place where his emerging thematic crisis is resolved. *Pocoangelini* is a character cycle in the modernist tradition of Pound and Eliot dealing with identity and tinged with irony. The sequence ends in a stalemate, which may account partially for the lack of critical attention that it has received.

Lewis Turco is a formalist, but not to the extent that formal concerns overshadow the dynamics of content. Rather, the poetry seeks a balance where an interplay occurs between the two elements, each heightening the effect of the other. This principle offers an entrance into the complex ideology that can be found in *The Inhabitant*. Representative pieces from Turco's most brilliant and critically acclaimed cycle resolve the conflict in the early work, mark a transition into another phase of his career, and stand as the cornerstone to all his latter writing. This cycle deserves an extended discussion.

The Inhabitant develops the metaphor of the house and nature and plays Walt Whitman's expansive, life-affirming poetic vision against Emily Dickinson's spare, dark poetry. These visions are embodied in the poetic forms that the two poets use. Rather than the stalemate of *Pocoangelini*, *The Inhabitant* ends with a remarkable transformation where oppositions are synthesized and the speaker finds unity in the world. The skillful use of metaphor in *The Inhabitant* makes it a remarkable document in post-1945 American Poetry.

For Turco, poems are structures of oppositions. *The Inhabitant* is constructed on the basis of two opposing verse forms that interact to create a necessary tension. The initial form begins with the first poem of the sequence, "The Door":

THE DOOR
On a sculpture by Ivan Albright

There is a door
made of faces
faces snakes and green moss

which to enter is
death or perhaps
life which to touch is

to sense beyond the
figures carved in
shades of flesh and emerald

the Inhabitant at home
in his dark
rooms his hours shadowed or

lamptouched and that door
must not be
attempted the moss disturbed nor

the coiling lichen approached
because once opened
the visitor must remain in

that place among the
Inhabitant's couches and
violets must be that man

in his house cohabiting
with the dark
wife her daughter or both.
(*Inhabitant* 11; *Shifting Web* 61)

It is made of short, often enjambed lines whose basic unit of composition is the word. Line length is determined by word count. The opposition starts in the second poem, "The Hallway" (*Inhabitant* 11, 13):

THE HALLWAY

The Inhabitant stands in his hallway. A long way from the door, still the gentleman has a distance to go before he can leave, or enter, or simply resume.

Here there is small illumination. The only window is of squares of stained glass, in the door behind him which is closed.

Things wait in the narrow aisle. Objects beguile him — each has its significance, in and beyond itself; each is an obstacle in a way to be touched and passed:

Touched and repassed, and with each touching to become more than the original substance. The Inhabitant stands in his hallway, curiosities looming ahead and behind.

It is as though, almost, this furniture had become organs, extensions of his body. If he listens, the gentleman may find his pulse booming in the hallseat, under the lid, gently, among artifacts and mathoms.

Let him proceed; let his footfall say *clum*, silence, *clum*. Let the stained light lie amber on a black umbrella in its stand, fall scarlet on the carpet, make a blue haze of a gray hatbrim rising in shadow to the level of his eye to rest on an iron antler in the hall.

The Inhabitant is home. Let him go down the hallway, choosing to pass the stair and banister this time, pass these things of his, levelly, moving from light to light, shadow to shadow.

In this verse the phrase or syntactic unit becomes the unit of composition. These clusters of words are strung together to create long breath lines.

These structural elements can be discussed without ever mentioning what is actually said in the poem. But going further, the opposing verse forms, without ever stating the fact, draw attention to two opposing ideologies as well as a dialectic which are central concerns of *The Inhabitant*.

Two strong and often conflicting poetics have had a huge impact on the nature of twentieth century American poetry. One is derived from the short lines of Emily Dickinson and is found in the work of William Carlos Williams and Robert Creeley. (Williams has been able to successfully synthesize the poetics of Whitman and Dickinson, but his debt to Dickinson is huge.) The other is a construction of longer lines which can be traced back to Walt Whitman and finds its way to the poetry of Robinson Jeffers, Allen Ginsberg, and many others.

Not only do Whitman and Dickinson represent different forms, they represent different ways of looking at human existence. Emily Dickinson's poetry has helped spark an idiosyncratic, despairing tendency in twentieth century American poetry. Traces of an existential philosophy are found in her poems. It is an ideology shared and expanded by the likes of Kierkegaard, Heidegger, Sartre and Derrida. Walt Whitman celebrates life and death, finding unity in existence rather than fragmentation. Indeed, he is so positive that his celebration of death ultimately becomes a denial. Although Whitman has had a profound impact on twentieth century poets in a formal sense, many poets have failed to share his positive vision. His view of being is shared with Hegel. The content of *The Inhabitant* clearly takes a Hegelian view of the world while its form places it within the context of a necessary dialectic. It must be remembered at this point that the ideology of the text may not be that of the author and may not be represented again in the body of the author's work. The text is essentially a closed system of language.

This identification with Hegel begins to explain the formal concern with oppositions in the piece. To examine the piece is to see clearly that *The Inhabitant* moves on carefully constructed subsystems of image repetitions. Again, these systems in the opposition to each other reflect the larger structure of the sequence. For example, "The Door" reveals the unfolding system. In stanzas two and three, two important oppositions stand out:

life : death
organic : inorganic

This list expands as the text progresses, and consequently possibilities for reading emerge:

reality : dreams
light : dark
man : woman
adulthood : childhood
being : nothingness

All these oppositions are embodied through the existence of the Inhabitant himself. The house exists through his perception. Thus, the most important oppositions arise between the objective and subjective worlds.

In the Hegelian sense, the objective and subjective worlds are dialectic. There is a seemingly irreconcilable opposition between the two, but in actuality they create a unity. To be human is to experience these oppositions and move through life from a finite to an infinite consciousness. These notions are exactly what *The Inhabitant* represents.

The poem is a representation of consciousness, not random, but interacting and developing. This consciousness is explained in Hegel's *The Phenomenology of Spirit* (Hegel 59). The image which mediates the relationship between the objective and subjective worlds in *The Inhabitant* is the mirror. As the Inhabitant moves through the world of experience varying reactions occur. At times there are intimations of unity, and at other times there is alienation and fear. But always, his moods and experiences are reflected in the concrete world of things. This does not imply a primacy of the subjective. It represents a necessary dialectic. Logically, the mirror is a perfect correlative for this concept. It is a paradoxical other which reflects an image.

As the consciousness of the Inhabitant changes and moves toward his ultimate unity, so does the mirror. It first appears as a passing reference in

THE HALLSEAT

only the gate guarded by
two stags on either
side of

the mirror where only one
hat ever hangs....
(*Inhabitant* 4)

Here the concern is not with the mirror, although it certainly contributes to the passage. The lines carry a mood of disjunction. The outside world is strange and not to be trusted. These moods are precisely what gives the poem its appeal; however, they are always changing, never static.

Mirrors are mentioned in "The Attic" where they meld with memorabilia and loneliness, "the toys mice play with; mirrors reflecting upon solitude; cords and scissors..." (*Inhabitant* 17, *Shifting Web* 63). It is important to note that thus far the mirrors have only been included in sequences of objects. No actual reflections have occurred, and the Inhabitant is split from his world.

In "The Bedroom" more attention is paid to the reflecting image. As with other things in the house, it is given human qualities, a reflection of the Inhabitant:

> The mirror on the morning wall listens as swelling waters speak darkly across the room. Two beacons converge and blend among drifting lamps and tables.
> (*Inhabitant* 39)

A momentary, lyric unity occurs as the world is absorbed into the metaphoric subjectivity of the Inhabitant's mind. Reality becomes a vacuum of unbalanced thought.

It is not until "The Bathroom" that an actual confrontation occurs with the mirror. In the opening stanza the Hegelian concept of evolving personality is stated. "The Inhabitant will emerge another man — the old one will diminish in steam and water hissing or bubbling in taps and bowls" (*Inhabitant* 43). This emergence is combined with a water/rebirth motif. The mirror is mentioned again in the fourth stanza: "In the mirror, under the comb's teeth, an effulgence emerges to gleam back at gaze" (*Inhabitant* 43). This passage mentions the mirror by name, but the whole poem occurs in front of it.

It is not at all surprising that a poem entitled "The Mirror" immediately follows "The Bathroom." A vision of disunity is presented in the first two stanzas:

> In the mirror this
> other the heart of glass
> brave beyond
> his agate eyes
>
> in them currents forever
> at their gaze look away
> catch him
> at a glance
> (*Inhabitant* 44)

The mirror serves to divide the personality. It presents the double so often alluded to in the postmodern text, a self independent from the subjective in the world of objects, yet a part of the self. But then a synthesis begins to emerge also. As much as the mirror image seems frightening and alien, it becomes a necessary step toward a realization of the unity between the two worlds:

> this creature of mercury
> make him stop staring out
> of himself
> into crystal so
>
> clear so foretelling that
> he can surely see floating
> in shallows
> the shoddy heart.
> (*Inhabitant* 44)

Subtly, the mood of the poem shifts to different concerns. The Inhabitant's desire is to stop the reflecting process, but the ever-present oppositional force arises too. He is fascinated with the image of himself as well as distressed and frightened. The synthesis that concludes the poem is beginning to emerge. The Inhabitant is taking steps toward the realization that the seemingly alien form is his and not to be feared. As much as he exists in the subjective, he is a concrete reality in the objective world too. In Blakean terms, the body and soul have been united.

As an afterthought, this particular idea occurs later in another short poem, "The Looking Glass." This acceptance of the reflection is much more serene; still, the importance of the mirror's linking power is not fully utilized:

> and there lying in
> its circle
>
> of smooth things the
> eye preens
>
> in its own vision
> before it
>
> rakes the wind again
> and rises
> (*Inhabitant* 56)

This particular consciousness, although it has taken steps toward self-realization, is still bound to an alienated attitude toward the objective world. In many a sense, this represents the postmodern ideology that Turco attempts to transcend. The mirror image is only a fragmentary truth.

The final poem in *The Inhabitant*, "The Dwelling House," is a well-constructed poem that brings the sequence to a sudden climax with the

Inhabitant's realization of the unity between the objective and subjective worlds. It is fittingly written in long Whitmanesque lines.

In this section Turco's fine use of linguistic structures and ideas are brought to a synthesis also. For after all, the text is a piece of writing, and ultimately that writing will reflect itself. For ideas to exist, they must exist in language.

The first section of "The Dwelling House" stays within the conventional boundaries that have been defined through the text. Only now, the Inhabitant has stepped into the actual world itself. All is well.

The third section, however, brings ominous tidings. The Inhabitant has trouble breaking free from his dreams. By the third section, "The dream stayed with him..." and some remarkable events begin to occur:

> A tree grew out of his doorstep, gray ribbons tangled in its branches. A trunk of steel sprang upward, and an explosion of metal limbs groped at the sky.
> (*Inhabitant* 64)

The Inhabitant appears to be consistent with the ideology of the postmodern text. Subjective potentiality is taking over completely; in fact, the Inhabitant seems to be drifting into a psychotic state. It seems he will never transcend the narrow limits of his own being and the sequence will be, in the end, static.

Actually, a completely different transformation is occurring because every action in the text has meaning. Every fragment is really a connected part of the whole which leads to the Inhabitant's realization of himself and his world. Objects are beginning to lose their distinctions as the oppositions merge. The metal tree is not a hallucination but a representation of the synthesis of the organic and inorganic which started the poem.

By the fourth section the synthesis is hardly deniable: "His eyes were the door itself when the fourth day broke" (Inhabitant 64). Language combines oppositions - "black sun" and "steel tree" as the tree grows, absorbing the known worlds into one world.

The mirror image occurs one last time at the close of the poem:

> He went to the door, naked; opened it; moved into the daylight where the world walked. With his eyes he met other eyes beyond the portal — men, women and children who knew his nakedness as he knew theirs.

> It was a true flesh the Inhabitant made to walk through the city: in each eye he saw the image folk saw in his.
> (*Inhabitant* 65)

It is a vision of complete closure. The objective world and the subjective world have been united. The Inhabitant *is* the mirror. As with Whitman, the possibility of representing this complete unity is problematic and not without its contradictions. But with a skillful manipulation of the mirror image throughout the text Turco has created a totality which is alive with meaning and transformation.

One of the great surprises in *The Shifting Web* is the selections from Turco's *American Still Lifes*, a relatively obscure volume. These lyrics mark the high point of the collection and follow *The Inhabitant* thematically. *The Inhabitant*'s achievement as a poetic cycle is its transformation. The lyrics in *American Still Lifes* takes us into that world only briefly glimpsed at the end of *The Inhabitant*. It is a transformed world, the product of an original voice that has at last found its own vocabulary and syntax. In one poem, "The Ice House," we are told, "The walls are of rough plank, / Time melts slowly in the straw / without reflection — / it is like dwale in glass" (*American Still Lifes* 44, *Shifting Web* 99). The boundaries have been opened and totality has been achieved where the oppositions in early poems now merge. Where once there was fragmentation there is now unity and wholeness. These poems seem at first to be devoid of humanity; but look closely, the reader will find humanity in nature.

In the representative pieces from *A Cage of Creatures* and *A Maze of Monsters*, Turco's writing goes through a gothic era. All these pieces in some way investigate archetypes of the horrible and fantastic. At their root, these poems are an acknowledgment of death and decay. No matter how metaphorically veiled, the dissipation of things haunts the house of *The Inhabitant* and these poems are that realization brought to fruition.

At the end of *The Shifting Web* is a healthy inclusion of new poems. Why, from his prolific output, did Turco select these particular poems? Nearly all the later poems reflect on the work of the past and the process of writing poems. The universal is made particular, and the poet finally reveals his own intentions to the reader who has become a trusted friend. One poem, "The Habitation," addresses thematic questions that have arisen in previous poems: "There is no way out. / Now the windows have begun / to cloud over: cobwebs, dust" (*Shifting Web* 168). The house, for him, is the body, which has made an uneasy peace with nature outside the doors and windows. These are intensely personal poems in which Turco also makes peace with American poetic tradition and takes his place in it.

Works Cited

Georg Wilhelm Friedrich Hegel, *The Essential Writings*, New York: Harper & Row, 1959.
Lewis Turco, *American Still Lifes*, Oswego: Mathom, 1981.
— , *Awaken, Bells Falling: Poems 1959-1967*, Columbia: University of Missouri, 1968.
— , *A Cage of Creatures*, Potsdam: Banjo, 1978.
— , *The Inhabitant*, Northampton: Despa, 1970.

— , *A Maze of Monsters*, Livingston: Livinston University, 1986.

— , *The New Book of Forms: A Handbook of Poetics*, Hanover: University Press of New England, 1986.

— , *Pocoangelini: A Fantography and Other Poems*, Northampton: Despa, 1971.

— , *The Public Poet*, Ashland: Ashland Poetry Press, 1991.

— , *The Shifting Web: New and Selected Poems*, Fayetteville: University of Arkansas, 1989.

— , *Visions and Revisions of American Poetry*, Fayetteville: University of Arkansas, 1986.

SINGING TO THE SAME TUNE,
BUT WITH DIFFERENT WORDS
Felix Stefanile

LEWIS TURCO HAS EARNED HIS REPUTATION NOT ONLY AS A POET, but as a scholar and a biographer. His books on poetry, its forms, and its prosody, are used in the schools. All of these gifts serve the poet in his latest collect, *A Book of Fears* [1998]. Mr. Turco's intellectual poise and stylistic grace are familiar to readers of poetry, but what makes this book a canny departure from his other work is the choice of personality types Mr. Turco presents to us. There is a touch of the psychological case study in Mr. Turco's offerings of "self portraits" this time.

The characters in A Book of Fears share, regardless of their varied lives, certain traits, moods and fears, certain preoccupations that mark them off from general society. What makes these lonely souls kin to each other is that they are all imprisoned by their obsessions, so that though they are distinct from each other as individuals, as far as the eye can see, they suffer the same disease, self-entrapment. Their hyper-attentiveness to their flaws, like the man who studies his approaching baldness with the fervor of a DNA-biologist, is the telltale sign of a spiritual malaise that assails them all:

PHALACROPHOBIA: The Fear of Balding

He washes his hair carefully in the shower,
massaging his scalp as gently as he can,
lathering twice, then working in conditioner,
rinsing at last. He sees it there afterward,
lying in the bottom of the tub —

a single strand of anguish, a filament
of rue. He picks it up and looks at it
accusingly. He turns the water off
and reaches for a towel. He dries himself
carefully, massaging his scalp as lightly

as he can. He looks into the mirror
over the sink and sees what he despairs
to see: the youngish man whose hairline even
in steam recedes almost from day to day,
whose eyes are wide with anguish and with rue.

He's washed his hair as carefully as he can,
lathering gently twice, rinsing at last
as though the man were father to the boy
he sees disappearing in steam and dream,
strand by strand, day by rueful day.

This gives to the poet's tone an underlay of familiar motifs, as if Mr.
Turco is singing to the same tune, but with different words.

My observation on this double thrust of difference with similarity
is, of course, only partly true, but the partliness I am speaking of is
essential to the construction of the poems, and gives them their family
resemblance. For instance, Mr. Turco patterns his syntax from character
to character in such a way that often, sonically — and in terms of breath
— the lyrics echo each other, and create a murmur that runs through
the book. This is what I mean by underlay. Perhaps Mr. Turco will
agree with me that often his syntax "rhymes" from page to page. In this
manner the poet is telling us something about his art, as well as about
the souls he is studying.

The gallery of portraits, of characters, is a traditional poetic mode,
of ancient lineage. Mr. Turco has given us his contributions to this form
in other books. *His Pocoangelini: A Fantography and Other Poems* (1973)

contains three sequences: "Pocoangelini," "The Sketches," and "Bordello." The "Pocoangelini" sequence, not related in theme to the other two sections, runs sixty-four pages, "Bordello," a mere ten. The three parts joined together in this way, unrelated as they are, give the book a jerry-built feeling, and my impression is that the superior poems in the collection deserved better editing. "Bordello" struck me as nothing new, a series of balladlike pieces dealing with men and women and sex, all perhaps a little too prettily, too literarily stated:

HANK FEDDER

Hank Fedder is my name. My wife is Maud
Fedder — she's a good woman, the neighbors
say. And she is, I guess. She's sure no bawd,
and that's God's truth. Goodness just about pours
out of her. Depends on what you call "good,"
of course. She's good in the house, out of doors,
at market, in her clubs — just anyplace.
Except in bed. There, she rubs my face

in the "dirt" she calls my "male mind." She makes
me sick of myself, of what I need to
do. She cuts my guts out, and then she takes
what's left of me, sets it in the window
like a dummy, calls it "Hubby," "Dad," bakes
cakes for it, and sends it off to work. Oh,
yes, she's good all right. She makes a fine spouse.
On her bridge night I come to this whorehouse

to salvage what's left of my need, of my
insides. It never works. I leave here done
to death with sickness, the sickness that I
have now, truly, just as she claims. She's won

her point. I'm not the man she married by
a long shot — no man at all. And my son,
our son...he knows it, hates the "hubby" of
that best of mothers he will always love.

"Pocoangelini" describes the spiritual journeying of a Quixote-like, Ariel-like, Adam-like character who undergoes a series of changes in a strange, dark, yet glittering world. Turco is a metrically skillful poet, and the Adam paradigm fits:

POCOANGELINI 12

She is caught in her frail house
as Poco is caught in his. The rib she stole
is the furniture of his breast. Poco puts
his ear to listen to the nameless Word
her lung suspires into blood, and the word
redounds, echoes out of the breath
of his own mouth.
                              Listen. She would have
seed of Pocoangelini. She would bring
more bone forth to walk among the walkers,
to chisel rimes upon monuments
in the fields among groves and grass —
the boudoir where lovers lie at last.

Elsewhere Pocoangelini has conversations with a mouse, with Mr. Earth, the moon, the mirror, a dandelion, and encounters various magical situations:

POCOANGELINI 5

Pocoangelini said,

"Lady, the bell is on my cap,
the cap is upon this head.
Womanhood wound in roses and ivy
shall never understand me."

To him she did reply,
"I have heard the bell upon your cap,
and, with my own eye,
sir, have I perceived its bobble.
It is a pretty bauble."

Then did Angelini shake
his sceptre into the blowing moon
there, where the trees make
spires of shadow into the night.
But his eyes were bright.

Sweet, the lady's laughter
rang to the bell's jangle. A bird,
caught in a limb, softer
echoed her joy out of the wood —
then he understood.

"Lady," did Poco cry,
"you misperceive my good intent
and the brightness of my eye.
My dance is light, the moon is pure,
this bell is not a lure!"

"Sir," then said the lady,
"though I may not apprehend you,
these are shadows, never ivy.
Let the bell sing, for the moon shows
that your sceptre is the rose."

Turco seems to have the whole of the English lyric tradition at his fingertips, and though this is not entirely a good thing — too much tinkle here and there, here a bit of Keats, there a bit of Mother Goose — I belong to the old school, and see in this bravura the commitment of a poet to craft. I trust poets who show clear influences, and I don't trust the groggy, toneless, "spontaneous" mutter of much that goes by the name of verse today among the younger, studiously untutored poets of the Confessional school. Many of the poems of the "Pocoangelini" sequence were first published in magazines like *Tri-Quarterly*, *Saturday Review*, and *Poetry*.

When I first read Pocoangelini in 1975 I would have liked to see Turco, who was an actively publishing poet as well as teacher — his *Poetry: An Introduction Through Writing* was one of the more original poetry texts on the market — return to the inspiration of "The Sketches," the sequence that formed the middle third of the book then under review. There, in a handful of character vignettes — A. R. Ammons called them "an autobiography of biographies" — we have a poet who is direct, clear-seeing, musical, and quite real. Poems like "Guido the Ice-House Man," "Ercole the Butcher," and "Mrs. Martino the Candy Store Lady" speak to the human condition with grace, always a strong point with Turco, and warmth. Just as important, I think the resistance of the subject matter — real people, often simple, not particularly highly endowed — works well with this poet's tendency to treat his material with too much "fanciness." A tension is set up between the nubbiness of the material and the neatness of Turco's technique:

GUIDO THE ICE HOUSE MAN

So what if it's hot in the sunny streets
    and the gang languishes after lunch
    and the morning games?
Down you go, boys, down you go,
    sluggish with warmth, to the ice-house shade.

170

When you come to the dreamy door
    that roars its silence in the sun;
    where the cubes of sawdust winter rest
    waiting for us to pick up chips
    for the salving of tongues —
When you come to that best of quiet doors,
    there Guido sits with his hat pulled down
    and his lids pulled down,
    and the shadows down, down to his knees
    like an awning's ghost —
Note no movement, not even his lips
    as Guido says, with his hat pulled down,
    "Welcome, you guys, come in, get cool.

"Get cool near the ice, boys," Guido says.

Precision of language, and to be envied.

A Book of Fears, however, points to social criticism of a strictly contemporary kind in which his biographer's eye for detail fixes on the milieus of advertising, fad, and the headlines of today for his imagery and discourse. Ours is a society of name brands, sexual idiom, victimology as hobby and so on. His poet's skill brings art to this spiritual squalor not as a praise for such matters, but as a new theme for poets to ponder. In other words, he does what serious poets always manage to do: he takes topic, and makes it theme. How far you wish to take Mr. Turco's journey into the quibbling maelstrom of contemporary sensibility is your business, but in his honor, his chamber music of up-to-date speech rhythms, his scholarly patience with the trivia and tragedy of twentieth-century urban life in the United States, this guide will tell you things you didn't think you knew.

"PAINT MIXED BY ANOTHER":
POEMS BY LEWIS TURCO AND EMILY DICKINSON
by Kathrine Varnes

> *What I put into words is no longer my*
> *possession. Possibility has opened. The future will forget,*
> *erase, or recollect and deconstruct every poem . . . . The*
> *conditions for poetry rest outside each life at a miraculous*
> *reach indifferent to worldly chronology.*
> —*Susan Howe,* My Emily Dickinson[1]

A NEW POEM IS HAUNTING ME LATELY. It's entitled "Crimson Children":

> Tonight the crimson children
> are playing in the west.
> They do not hear the stars call
> down the burning sky
> that time has passed, is passing
> under clouds afire,
> tumultuous with ash.

At first, the opening lines appear merely a flowery way to describe sunset. But "crimson children" has an ominous feel. I wonder how they got red. A burning sky could be a second metaphor for sunset, extended with "clouds afire," but by the time we reach "tumultuous with ash," even if the children are metaphorical, they seem burdened, deafened by fire, or perhaps by play. How frightening — how apt — it is to equate the two. We have all played like that.

In the introduction to *Emily Dickinson, Woman of Letters: Poems and Centos from Lines in Emily Dickinson's Letters*, Lewis Turco mentions that at a reading of these poems an audience member accused him of "tampering with an American classic." This phrase pestered me as I read and re-read the series titled *A Sampler of Hours*, but not because I think it a fair charge. Turco replies that only Dickinson's poems comprise the "classic" canon of her writings, and that he refashioned materials from her letters instead, which very few people read, in order to give them more light. But perhaps Lew is too modest here. In transforming excerpts from the letters into poems, he's not only creating poetry, he's also creating criticism. No doubt this *is* tampering, but no more outrageous than what any thinking reader of Dickinson already does with the poems. Dickinson herself presents no fewer multitudes than Whitman. Margaret Dickie makes this case in *Lyric Contingencies* when she points out how often the positions of Dickinson's poems shift and contradict each other.[2] The poem, "The Deep Stranger" makes a similar case:

> Sometimes as I am drifting
> toward my sleep, I dream
> I am the deep stranger
> smoking his pipe, looking
> through his reading glasses,
> and sometimes I look out and see
> I am not dreaming.

Reading these poems, we don't know where Dickinson ends and Turco begins. This poem gives us an interior voice — one we might presume is Dickinson's — becoming aware of another presence — one we might presume is Turco. The poem offers a way of understanding such a dual authorship, a dream that is not one. It also suggests a fluidity of identity between centuries, gender, states of consciousness. If this is tampering, it is the postmodern sort: playful, expansive, thoughtful, a simultaneous mixture of art and criticism. Of course, the criticism tends toward the understated, but it underpins the project and each poem.

Unapologetic tampering with the poet and her life is the work of many a critic. How else to put her holographic works into type? She's called an enigma, and yet — despite the many complaints — we know so much about her: reading habits, bread baking, wardrobe. This is more than most of us know about our distant relatives. We speculate on her affairs, if any, with men or women. We pry and pry, looking for some unturned ground to expand the growing landscape of Dickinson Studies, as motley and as vigorous as traditional boxwood next to a patch of sprawling nasturtiums and sweet peas. The impulse to protect her — what? Reputation? Privacy? Purity? Organic Integrity? — persists in a rather sexist stereotype of the frail poet whispering by in a white gown. But Dickinson's power needs no protection. Her sturdy language invites entanglement, challenge, enough to inspire Sheila Coghill and Thom Tammaro to collect *Visiting Emily: Poems Inspired by the Life and Work of Emily Dickinson*, an anthology compiled from nearly eighty poets from Robert Bly to Amy Clampitt, Billy Collins to Maureen Owen,[3] as well as the earlier compilation *ED: Letters from the World* edited by Marguerite Harris,[4] not to mention the many poets outside either anthology.[5] With so many poets claiming her as an influence, poets from such different aesthetic and political persuasions, we must admit that her words cry out to be used again and again. When someone cries foul, the objection probably derives from a fragile understanding of the "classic" in question. For it is only through extensive tampering that authors become classic in the first place.

Turco's felicitous tampering — the most ambitious project using Dickinson's language that I've encountered — reveals a new Dickinson, or at least one I hadn't met before, despite having read the letters.[6] We know Dickinson of the dashes and seemingly erratic capitalizations, the hymnal patterns broken against off-rhyme and worrying, earth-shattering metaphor. The woman of letters to whom Turco introduces us appears more relaxed, although still in lines. "Crimson Children," for instance, has an easy three beat line with variations in the rhythm that snaps shut with the barely there off-rhyme of west/ash ending the poem. His arranging of her language, interleaved with his own, highlights what he calls in his introduction "abstract syntax," a writer's version of abstract expressionism in painting. As he explains, "What one is really doing with words when one employs abstract syntax is manipulating connotations, associations and overtones, and not primary meanings, denotations" (4). He calls this a modernist project. One could also see it as postmodernist in the way it creates a new Dickinson through a blended authorship across the centuries. For, although he works to assimilate Dickinson's style, the poems are a collaboration, as much his as hers. After all, the poems have *titles*. These don't always seem necessary to the poems, as with the lovely "Nocturne," for instance, which runs

> This is the world that opens and shuts
>   like the eye of the wax doll
>   lying in a box
> of cast-off things. I hear its breath
>   in the wind of evening,
>
>   in the darkness between planets
>   and the shining of the stars,
>   even the whistle
> of a boy passing late at night,
>   or the low of a bird.

But the title doesn't hinder our reveling in those quick flights from cast-off doll's eye to the space between planets to a boy's whistle. With other poems, such as "The Amherst Fire," we'd be uncertain how much of the poem to take metaphorically without the assistance.

I sprang to the window and each
side of the curtain saw that awful
sun. The moon was shining high and the birds

singing like trumpets, and so much
brighter than day was it that I saw
a caterpillar measure a leaf far

down in the orchard. The innocent
dew was falling and sweet frogs prattling
in the dark pools as if there were no earth.

What, indeed, is Earth but a nest
from whose rim we are all falling?

Discussing the poems keeps one wary; it's impossible to refer to *the?* author without stumbling over number and gender. A little New Critical discipline comes in handy, if one refers to the poem, not to the authorship. The only way to indulge in the pursuit of intention would be to tease out who penned what, thus violating the spirit of the entire project. Any impulse to use identity as a shortcut to the poem goes unencouraged. So, while it's clear that "I sprang to the window" must represent the historical Dickinson waking to the Amherst fire, it functions as dramatic monologue realized by the consistency of observation in the poem, the heightened awareness of "that awful/sun" and "birds//singing like trumpets." The poem makes this clear by specifying "that I saw/a caterpillar measure a leaf far//down in the orchard." That is, *I saw* — with all its attendant possible meanings — is the heart of the poem. The shift to the last two lines makes one of the most overt possible nods in the series to its joint authorship. It *might* be a Dickinsonian commentary on the frogs' speculations. But it might also be the voice of our contemporary poet, linking the historical

176

moment of the fire with our own, pulling back the camera to admit a wider view. It shows we are all falling.

Thematically, the poems keep to material not too far afield for readers of Dickinson's work. More than half of the poems address time's passing or death via the seasons, a rough third of the poems make use of the contrast between outer and inner worlds. The remaining describe domestic scenes, loneliness, god, poetry. One comes close to downright sexy.

What I found remarkable, in terms of a common strain in the series, is how often the poems (by my count all but four in the series) centered on sound. But I was startled by how musically, how precisely, some of the attention to sound was actually an attendance to its absence. In "The Naked Eye," for instance, a delightful series of surprising images are described for the inevitably missing "you." In the fourth stanza, we learn that "The cat walking down the stair/makes a great noise—the banister/bulges out as she descends." That looks like the hyperbole that intimacy allows. In the last stanza, however, we're told that "The candles speak so slightly that/we can hardly hear their words." This unheard, or hardly heard, sound is less of an exaggeration, more of an unusual accuracy, and the contrast with the preceding intimacy gives the poem a sudden feeling of loneliness. The flickering candles converse, but we are left out of the conversation and have no conversation of our own to distract us. A charming second example occurs in "Summer's Chariot":

Summer is past and gone;
Autumn with the sere and yellow leaf
is already upon us.

Someone must have oiled
his chariot wheels, for I did not
hear him pass.

In order to imagine not hearing the chariot wheels, one must first imagine them squeaking, then absent them. Likewise, we are left largely to our imaginations when trying to hear enough of the following question from "Death" to answer it: "When you hear the new violet sucking/her way among the sods, shall you//be resolute?" The dazzle of the visual images and abstract logic initially make these non-sound sounds less apparent, but the steady insistence on audibility in so many registers — the persistent play of bird songs, crickets, flies buzzing, wind, echoing bells, voices in whispers and shouts, the final ticking of the clock in the closing poem — is what binds the poetry beyond its origins with a gifted poet and pianist. Whether this focus on sound comes to us in Dickinson's original language or not, we know Turco has made the selections, arrangements, and augmentations. One cannot believe it a coincidence that Turco put into his subtitle three terms often used to describe music.

Aside from the titles, the arrangement of the poems on the page, often with three stages of indentations, is an obvious addition to Emily Dickinson's repertoire. She tended to left-justify her longhand. The visual signal aligns these poems more with the tradition of William Carlos Williams and the inscrutable variable foot of free verse. Consider "May, Merely":

> The weeds pant
> like the center of summer.
> I follow my nose
> to the dogwood in bloom:

> It is May
> merely, but Amherst blossoms
> in the early heat,
> sap oozes from the bark,

and the limbs
are heavy with what may be
phantom fruit, the seed
in the dusty pollen.

This is far from hymnal stanza — and yet. We do have a steady visual pattern, and the words seem to fall into a two beat rhythm, broken most noticeably by the first lines in the second and third stanzas. When we get to "May/merely," the alliteration encourages us to keep them in a two-beat unit (scandalously) across the line break. The eighth and eleventh lines have three beats, no doubt due to all that oozing and fruiting. Such is the playful yet serious trespass of the poem — on top of summer procreation in the spring.

Seasons (or people) not quite behaving as they ought is another pattern in the poems. In "First Snow," the weather seems timely, but the narrator must work hard to understand the relationship between autumn and winter, remarking, "I remember the leaves were falling,/and now there are falling snows./Are not leaves the breathren of snows?" The image in the last stanza recalls that famous William Carlos Williams poem:

I dream of being a grandam
and binding my silver hairs,
the children dancing around me.

No, she isn't dancing naked as the genius of her home, but she indulges in a similar kind of abandon, a relinquishing of the seasons before winter. Both poems celebrate age, the body as it is. Both play with the idea of an alternative, archetypal self. I don't mind if this isn't the "real" Dickinson. I like believing it might be.

In "Poetry," what Turco describes as a found poem that collects snippets from Dickinson's letters on her craft, a middle stanza appears to comment on the *Sampler of Hours* project:

> I marked a line in one
> verse, because I met it after I
> made it and never consciously touch
> a paint mixed by another person. I do
> not let go of it, because it is mine.

Although Dickinson does not consciously touch a paint mixed by another, when she sees her phrase elsewhere, she refuses to relinquish her claim. Turco is clearly up to his elbows in Dickinson's paints; that's plain. His investment is also conscious. Nevertheless, he claims his poet's rights to her legacy, just as feminist poet and scholar Susan Howe once possessively indicated in the title of her book, *My Emily Dickinson*. Elliptical and detailed at once, Howe's book revolutionized for many how to understand Dickinson as an innovative, modernist poet akin to Stein. Perhaps more importantly, it approached the subject with an artist's passion and personal investment. *A Sampler of Hours* does this as well with less fanfare. Poets in English of any country, but particularly American poets, must come to terms with Emily Dickinson. Most try. But not every poet can tamper with her paint box, come away with a prize, colors still on his sleeves, and live to tell about it.

[1] Berkeley: North Atlantic Books, 1985. p. 13.

[2] *Lyric Contingencies: Emily Dickinson and Wallace Stevens.* Philadelphia, U Penn P, 1991.

[3] Iowa City: U of Iowa P, 2000.

[4] New York: Corinth Books, 1971.

[5] For an updated list, see the website maintained by Elizabeth Aracic. "Poems about Emily Dickinson: a list of poems to and about Emily Dickinson published in the last 100 years." *Titanic Operas: A Poets' Corner of Responses to Dickinson's Legacy.* Ed. Martha Nell Smith. 1999-present. <http://www.iath.virginia.edu/dickinson/titanic/aracic.html>

[6] I should mention *Tea With Emily*, a one-act play by Martha Furey based on Dickinson's letters. It doesn't strike me as ambitious, however, since it attempts to represent her rather than represent *with* her.

Acknowledgments & Tributes

Dad

As I go around in the odd, anxious, half-awake state of an infant's mother, or lie in Grandmother's Maine farmhouse bedroom listening to the birds fly in and out the hole behind my head, I seek out recollections of my father. We came here when I was just weeks old, and forty years later we are together again, separated only by a quarter mile of family meadow, brook and trees. How shall I describe him?

He isn't a man of half-measures. He may be experienced thoroughly angry, enormously pleased, totally disgusted, completely engaged in heated debate, wrestling a child down amidst gales of giggles, or tapping out reams of writings in the room overhead—but never multitasking, never partially one place and partially another.

Looking back, our lives seem to be in a book. I was surrounded by all sorts of words and wordplay: rhyme, rhythm, spondee, anapest, allegory, alliteration . . . mother's favorite place is in the corner reading, while father's favorite place is writing. When he takes little Phoebe on his knee (just as he did Christopher, Jessie, me, and any other child within reach), he says "This is the way the lady rides/ta trot ta trot ta trot ta trot/This is the way the gentleman rides/ta gallop ta gallop ta gallop ta gallop . . ." on and on, until finally the jockey goes . . . (moments of delighted anticipation pass until finally we go) "WHOOP!" and we slide down the leg, laughing, gasping. Then back on the knee we go, and it's "Bumpety bumpety bump/My name is Mortimer Lump/I eat out of pans and old tin cans/Because I live in a dump, a dump/Because I live in a dump!" (When I ran a library baby hour, I couldn't resist the urge to lead my moms and kiddies through this ritual, always accompanied by an apology and explanation that my poet Dad had made it up).

I know that I wrote a villanelle, but I don't have it in my head. Early fragments of my writing that do remain are these:

There's a war in Cambodia
A war in Vietnam
Instead of loving people
We love the atom bomb

and

The wind, the wind, oh how it blows
Over the treetops in a dancing pose
Around and around and around it swirls
And when it stops, it twirls and twirls

I remember Dad, looking a little like Sonny Bono in a leather fringy vest. I remember Dad, shocked and sobbing in front of the TV the day JFK died. I remember Dad, reading nursery rhymes aloud to me. I remember the annual

Christmas Tree Expedition:

December Market

We leave two black strips on the road behind us
heading up the tall hill in the brown and green Plymouth
for the annual trip to the Orchard Store
pulling into the parking lot carefully so as not to
hit any toddlers, grampas, or people pulling trees.
I am sure all the good ones are gone, but Mom
finds a puffy round one with a crooked top
that will drive Dad crazy but looks nice anyway.
Inside, there are bins of apples: Granny Smith, Cortland, Macs
and birdseed, ornaments, dog food, vegetables, chestnuts, candy.
Bread and cookies stock shelves lined with wreaths and Santas.
Coolers are filled with cider, cheese, and meat. I like cheddar.

The girl at the counter writes everything down on a
paper bag and adds it up by hand. She dumps
apples out of the basket into another bag.

Outside, Dad is still trying to put the tree on top
of the car. He grumbles. It gets shoved into
the trunk; some branches fall off.
We are headed back down the hill, to eat
and dream, and make cookies,
and put tinsel on our crooked tree.
I remember Dad The Avenger, swooping down the street in the
green Plymouth
Fury I disaffectionately nicknamed "Jaws" during my rebellious teen
years.

Swimming

There was a smell of pine trees
and our bodies as we ran
down thicketed banks, to the river
whose currents swept and eddied
under the metal bridge. We dove in
and were swept downstream, grabbing
at thick ropes tied to trestles, laughing
as the vortex tugged, fought,
twisted us around,
tore our hands loose
and plunged us down
to softest mud that gripped us.
We struggled, and our lungs
urged against closed mouths for liquid breath
(white stars illuminating clenched eyelids)
until, freed, we burst back into air and sun, then
climbed bare-legged and wet through brambles
back to the road, and home for dinner.

I remember Dad's music—the long reels of tape he'd mix from big piles
of records of various kinds: Classical, barbershop, brass, folk, rock (the
last two, I coveted, especially Melanie). I remember Dad just once
saying "Don't read that book," and of course I secretly did, then
wondered what was so great about its hundreds of pages. I remember

Dad, looking sadly philosophical at the funeral of a mother who annoyed, yet seemingly also inspired him in complex ways.

I think of my own name, his choice, Melora. People have a wide variety of responses to it, usually involving a misspelling or mispronunciation. "Oh, that's pretty, where's it come from?" is probably the most frequent comment. "An epic poem about the Civil War called 'John Brown's Body' by Stephen Vincent Benet" I reply. (If I'm in the mood, I add "Dad wanted to name me Gergrundehyde, and Mom wanted to name me Julie — so they compromised").

However, my favorite story about my name tells his mother's reaction when she first heard it: "Oh, thank you for naming her after me!" she said, and his jaw dropped to the floor in a rare speechless moment, as he realized that his mother's name, May Laura, and that of me, his infant daughter, were disconcertingly alike.

I remember trips to Pemaquid Beach on hot Maine summer days:

Sandcastles

Father carries our yellow pail
down to where the waves reach,
dips deep into bluegreen seafoam,
carries it back, sloshing,
(strong black-haired legs all wet),
and empties it into our castle moat.

Mixing just the right combination
of sand and water, his fingers dribble
fanciful towers fashioned unbelievably high:
windows into caverns where fair maidens
await their heroes' rescues from dragons,
and dungeons are hidden, monsters
safely imprisoned by salt, sea air,
bright sun, and clear sky.

I recall the years I spent as his writing student at the State University of New York College at Oswego. There were wonderful instances when I had written well or spoken well in class; there were terrifying moments when I felt I hadn't accomplished what I should; there were anxious times when I felt different, somehow isolated from the other students; above all, there was awe of—and pride in—my talented, daunting, funny, brilliant, accomplished father.

Now that we have come full circle, I sometimes worry about him and his health, as he has worried about me. I watch him play with my daughters or joke with my stepdaughter. Later on, I hear my poet/librarian husband read rhymes to our child, and the present blends with the past, sleep with waking, imagination with memory.

Untitled

The Phoenix has been known
to rise from the ashes
bright feathers dulled by the cold
that follows such intense heat
bones weary from hovering
over bleak earth for so long

She watches dusk cling to day
and evening slip into grateful sleep
but 4 am arrives, and the blaze
clears away her cluttered nest
leaving her with the moon, the stars
and a brown field to sweep clean

—Melora Ranney Norman, née Turco

Valentine's Day, 2004

EPISTLE 7: Lewis Turco

Lewis, I'll write this letter
& never send it. I'll share it with strangers, but not you.
What I must say concerns things so long ago it almost seems better
to keep silent, but I still long for the closure found in the last
line of a poem. Or do I dread it? You retired from
SUNY Oswego and profess no more 'neath the nuclear reactor
on blue Ontario's shore. U dun yer time. You survived in the art of writing
lines, which is more than most, more than me. My re(a)d comrades count
me among the walking dead or M.I.A. I avoid them elaborately.

A forgotten anthology of verse contains "A Constellation of Poets."
Don't worry. You're there in the heavens, but relegated to a nether region
near a black hole. If you're fortunate enough to be blessed as minor,
I suppose your disciples never had a prayer. But then, you found me; I
never looked for you. How surprised I was one May afternoon, an
undergraduate (not at your school), to receive a letter from a real poet
praising work I had submitted to a magazine. (I thought what I'd written
was fiction, but easily changed my mind when you called it poetry.)
You asked permission to reprint my thing in an anthology.
I danced in the rain with long-gone, blond Laura. You wouldn't
have liked me then, but you only knew me through letters (no doubt
deconstructing in some archive). I doubt you'd like me any better now.

We were mismatched from the start. I was in need of direction; I
suppose you needed Christian soldiers. Things went well for a time &
I appeared worthy. (You had others too, I know. (I sound
like a jealous wife.) When I started to fail you stood by me. Why?
I shudder whenever I recall the day my father took me to your house,
unannounced. I had just graduated with an advanced degree, a death
sentence that left me unemployable. He begged you to find me work. Even
Lew the Turk couldn't perform that miracle. You were tolerant of
my infatuation with the Black Mountain School, polite about
my flirtation with L=A=N=G=U=A=G=E and the marginal fringe.
Even though you must have abhorred it, you wrote a positive review of my
incoherent *Ourang-Outang.* What held us together was our obsession
with form, recognizing it as more than a parlor game of syllables & rhymes.

As the proper Mr. Booth once said, "There are many roads to Jerusalem."
By the sweat of my brow I labored to pay the debt on bills overdue.
("Some of you will turn out as critics," said Mr. Carruth.)

As for the closure (hurry up please, it's time): I apologize for being
a bad son, if that's what it was. (I still feel guilty about not
showing up at your house for dinner that night & never explaining.)
I don't blame you for drawing me into poesy, where I had no
business going. I had to go somewhere. Anyway, the joke was
on them, & it's a GREAT place to meet women. Sometimes
sons rebel against a father's iron will. I needed a lousy father. (Creeley
and Logan were *really* lousy fathers.) A man might leave his home
on a sunlit June morning only to have a piano come crashing down
on his head. I doubt, if he were allowed a final thought, he'd begrudge
the circumstances and people that led him to that place on the sidewalk
at that exact time. He'd think about something else, maybe taxes.
Between you and me all accounts are settled, the books are closed.

—De Villo Sloan

Pipe Smoke, Bullwhips, Bongos, and Bail: Remembering Lew Turco

Even though Lew Turco lived on West Eighth Street and shopped in my father's grocery store (Wilson's Market, which used to be on the corner of West Eighth and Oneida Streets), I had never actually met Lew until I went looking for him one day in his old office in the basement of Sheldon Hall. I had been readmitted to SUNY Oswego, and I burned with an ardor to learn about and to write poetry. Being on campus alone with nothing but hope and a registration slip, of course, I was excited, nervous, and a little intimidated. The Sheldon Hall janitor pointed out the way, saying, "Just follow the pipe smoke."

I did and found Lew behind his desk at work. He dropped what he was doing, and we spoke of poets and poetry. I told him I wanted to be a poet, that I burned to read it all. I believe I said something quasi-dumb, quasi-insightful like, "You know, and be well-read, just like T. S. Eliot." He told me to calm down, take my time, and read things in sequences. He said you'll go as far as you take yourself. He was right.

I remember the bullwhip coming out when we weren't up to snuff. I remember the bongos coming out to teach us iambs and trochees. I remember the obscene limericks (spoken off-campus, of course!), and I remember the thrill it was to do well and to earn his respect. I remember the humor and passion that he took to each class. When something was great or delightful, his face lit up. And did any of our professors wring more joy out of words themselves, especially the very roots of them? Of course, I mean the puns. I recall once when he punned and I punned on his pun. His face lit up in appreciation. But he jokingly said, "Okay. Murabito. That's enough. I'll handle the puns around here." Of course, I couldn't resist punning once more during that class, just to bust his chops. Those were classes. That was absolute immersion in language.

But three stories stand out the most. In one, I am a "cool," long-haired student in his advanced poetry class. I am in love with the long Whitmanesque line. I have just eaten a full dinner at my grandmother's house on Gregory Street. And I am smoking a Camel when we read my poem. The lines are everywhere. Turco checks his anger, his face turning red. He wants to know my thinking, my line rationale. "I don't know, Lew," I tell him stupidly, exhaling smoke, "they just came out that way."

I am sure that before him he saw an A student gone to the dogs of doggerel. Now, his face was crimson. "Murabito!" he howled, "shit just comes out that way! You're a poet! You ought to know every reason behind every line you write." Then I explained myself in terms of line length, break, parallelism, and so on. I knew that he expected something of me and was in no way going to let me sit there pontificating, and in the long run, letting myself down. I remember the night. I remember the poem. I remember the lesson. I teach the same "line rationale" lessons to my own students at Pitt, and it especially hits home when we are doing a poem by Lew Turco, who is, by the way, one of America's best writers of heterosyllabic verse.

In the second story, I am a troubled young man. I did a stupid thing and was arrested. I went to Lew to seek advice. After a brief conversation, he simply rose, said, "Stay here," and left his office. He returned about thirty minutes later. He had gone to speak on my behalf. He had truly and genuinely helped me in a way that went miles beyond his call of duty.

In the third story, I am a tenured professor myself, returning in 2002 to SUNY Oswego to be a visiting lecturer/reader. Lew Turco hears about it and is there. That means the world to me. Later that night, he joins me and my family for dinner at Vona's. At the bar, we both make the same pun at the same time. We burst out laughing.

When I think of Lew Turco, I think of a professor who was there with and for me in virtually everything I did as a student writer. And when I teach his ideas and poetry to my own students, I feel his lasting presence, and I hear the last words of his great poem "The Pilot": "I am with you still."

Happy Birthday, Lew

—Stephen Murabito

RUBLIW FOR LEWIS TURCO

Dear Lew,
I thought a few
lines in order here to
note I've not forgotten what you
taught, or what I learned, at least, then so clue-
less, but eager. Now, finding beau-
ty in new forms, I brew
a true rubliw
for you.

Matthew J. Spireng

Matthew J. Spireng was a math major at Clarkson College of Technology when Lew Turco, then teaching at SUNY Potsdam, awakened him to poetry. Spireng went on to get a master's degree in creative writing at Hollins College and, after a long hiatus, began writing poetry again in 1989. Since then, over 350 of his poems have appeared in journals across the U.S. His Inspiration Point won the 2000 Bright Hill Press Poetry Chapbook Competition. The above poem previously appeared in *The Hampden-Sydney Poetry Review*.

My first introduction to Lew was at the Poetry Forum at Fenn College, now Cleveland State. I had just moved to Ohio from Birmingham Alabama. Newcomer to poetry after a half-hearted painting career, I decided to venture down to the forum and try out a few poems. I dropped my name in a basket by the door and walked in expecting a small group of readers and friends. Wrong! No smattering of people. Instead, a large and lively crowd celebrating guest speakers topped off by an AME Zion Church choir singing spirituals. *This Little Light of Mine, I wish I Knew How I'd Feel To Be Free, There Is No Hiding Place Down Here*—exuberant rhythms I grew up longing to listen to over and over, so much so my friends and I would crawl under revival tents whenever we found a chance to slip away from the starchy Episcopal Church. As the singers left the stage, I lost myself in applause. A thought ballooned, "Not an act I'd like to follow."

Then came Lew's voice over the mike, "We'll start the poetry readings with Julie Suk from Birmingham Alabama. Will you please step up to the mike, Julie."

Mind you, this was during the time Martin Luther King was incarcerated in the Birmingham jail, the time Freedom Riders were attacked by police dogs and hosed down by the notorious Bull Conner. With my politically incorrect address and heavy drawl, I did not expect roses strewn at my feet. I did not expect those feet ever to reach the lectern, nor did I expect to survive humiliation. But somehow, with shaky voice and hands, I made it through the ordeal. Silence.

Then Lew jumped up, grabbed the poem, and read it again, giving it a lot more than the poem itself gave. The title? Long forgotten but no matter, Lew rescued me, and thereafter I became a regular along with Loring Williams, Alberta Turner, Russell Atkins, d.a.levy, Russ Salamon, Stuart Friebert, Mary Oliver, Bill McLaughlin, James and Mary Ann Magner, Dave French, Al Cahen, Grace Butcher—some of the names I remember when I sneak now under that flap of memory.

BOUND AS I AM

Mars
a deep crimson
floating low.
An exhilaration of fireflies
and stars
embossed on black.

Black
becoming to those of us
preparing to go out.

Late, warns the night,
time to leave.

No, not ready,
bound as I am
to the butterfly bush,
the zinnias, azaleas, and phlox,
and you who cut
and trim my life.

The darkened hedge, an altar
under a chalice of stars,
particles and waves
pouring around me--
a communion I want to share.

Will it hurt?
Will it rend
deeper than desire?

Desire kneels close
praying I won't let go.

—Julie Suk

Julie Suk is the author of four volumes of poetry, and co-editor of the anthology, *Bear Crossings*. Her collection, *The Angel of Obsession*, was a winner of the University of Arkansas Poetry Competition, and also won The North Carolina Roanoke-Chowan Award. Her most recent book, *The Dark Takes Aim*, was published in 2003 by Autumn House Press. Suk's work has appeared in numerous magazines and anthologies including *The POETRY Anthology, 1912-2002*.

Book of Forms
(A tribute to Wesli Court's "Western Wind"
— found on pages 157-8 in your *Book of Forms*)

Book of Forms, when will you stop
Cursing me from my bookcase?
Did I not give my pint of blood
In Turco's classroom embrace?
                    -Matt Jablonowski
                    (not as anonymous as you'd like…)

Book of Forms when will you stop?
Should I just hail a traffic cop
To cease this endless mockery?
When will you ever let me be
The rhyming fool whose lyrics drop?
Book of Forms, when will you stop

Cursing me from my bookcase?
Try like hell, I just can't erase
The agony of my mistakes;
Can't you hear my heart? It breaks!
For I see Lew Turco's angry face
Cursing me from my bookcase.

Did I not give my pint of blood?
I fancy myself quite the stud
Of writing syllables and rhymes.
Should be published in the *New York Times*!
But no, I sit six feet deep in mud.
Did I not give my pint of blood?

In Turco's classroom embrace
Whose wit and wisdom could replace

Mine? Nobody's, and that's for sure.
Let's get real, that's horse manure.
I dream I wear leather and lace
In Turco's classroom embrace.

I had the incredible good fortune to be a student of Dr. Turco's from my sophomore year until the end of my junior year, EWA 205 – 405. I also had the joy of being in the same group as Ben Doyle, Reginald Kornegay and many others. Dr. Turco gave me some good advice once. He said, "Matt, quit school and go into comedy." I didn't. Look where I am now. Happy Birthday, Dr. Turco.

—Matt Jablonowski, Oswego '94

LIVING WITH RACCOONS

The black-masked bandit
hunched on redwood sucks
the bones hugged close

from last night's hen   he
scavenges through his domain

                    the garden
pantry   No amount
of wild screams

or flailing fishnets
    does the work of one
            sure bullet or so

 the neighbors say

they call him "pest"
    and want me out

setting traps or lying

in the brush
for him and his small

family of three which lives

below the house
and raids the cans each Wednesday

late when lights are out
and chomping down the hill

the garbage grinders
crash and roll—

I have not killed
the rhythm of the night

        nor tipped the scales
in this unseemly war

I do not judge his sentence
light   Oh, let the bugger eat
if he will!   The goldfish

have been warned: DO NOT

swim up   to little paws

                        Stephen J. Herman

Lew taught me that a poem lives on many levels, all equally important. He taught me how to balance sound with idea and image. He taught me the craft and also a way to listen to my own inner voice.

Happy Birthday, Lew. Many thanks.

Stephen J. Herman received his B.A. in English (with honors) from the State University of New York at Oswego in 1969. He received his M.F.A. (in poetry) from the University of Massachusetts at Amherst in 1971. He has taught poetry and English at the City College of San Francisco, where he has served as Dean of Administrative Services since 1982. He also served as Human Rights Commissioner for the city and county of San Francisco from 1998 until 2000.

THE ARRIVAL

For Lew

And then time spread like a voice urgent and vestal
rippled to a mortise of wild plum and hazel
fields sparse and stony with broad thistle
thrust up a temple a tenement of limestone
spilt to an estuary of birdsong
commingling with the first june rain
finch bowers thrust into a tempest of being.

Here is a polestar, comets, the first raw yearnings
trees that grow solitary and those that delight in shade
gold canopy of thunder illumes for the first
dynamic rolled poise of night–day–night
startles a scarlet ibis impressed by the toeprint
of hominid in yellow clay ten days' walk from anywhere
on the thrusting bank of sea showered by the waters
where the boatman of dawn first set his oar.

—Gary A. Baker

SETANTA ("the little")

For Sheila

after the small rain
the oak begs with its root threads
at the hairpin turn of river
become a cassis trickle
the world a clutch of trees
in a checkerboard square

in all directions
a fraction of dust
mars Cassiopeia's Chair

—Gary A. Baker

Gary A. Baker first surrendered to the vitality and beauty of poetry in Lewis Turco's classroom some ten years ago. Although he concurrently yielded to the temptations of science, chemistry in particular, he continues to write and recalls fondly the impact Lew's animated lectures had both academically and personally. He is currently a Frederick Reines Fellow at Los Alamos National Laboratory in Los Alamos, NM where he lives with his wife Sheila and daughter Kali.

Recollections Of Lew

Lew Turco. Isn't he that crusty guy who puns a lot
and wrote the famous poem:
"Four Barbershop Quartets"?

I can't count the times I've told anyone who would listen about Lew's
singular neurological condition – aye eeee – that he can repeat
backwards any line you can throw at him. But not just repeat the words
in reverse order. He can, (or used to be able to, I swear), also reverse
the spelling of each word, starting with the last word in the line [enil
eht ni drow tsal eht]and then spit it at you. And that's not to mention
– no, I won't mention that. But sort of seriously, I do remember, with
fondness, the time that William Meredith came to visit a workshop Lew
was teaching. The next day Lew told me that later that night he'd asked
Meredith if there were any poets in the workshop and Meredith had
said – yeah, that guy Morton, but you'd better tell him he needs to
learn how to pronounce the word *internecine* properly. Lew probably
told the same thing to everyone in the class, sans the pronunciation
lesson. But it made me feel great then, and still does.

I haven't seen him for a while, over a decade, I'd guess.
But what's a decade among friends.
Happy Birthday, Lew.

—Dennis Morton

Dennis Morton

Father. Grandfather. Bankrupt grocer.
Failure isn't all it's cut out to be.
Now I work with 'at-risk' kids
and for California Poets In The Schools.
I write movie reviews for public radio (KUSP)
and the local daily.
I'm a co-host of *The Poetry Show* on KUSP –
the second oldest radio show in the country
devoted solely to poetry.
Several years ago I founded *Poetry Santa Cruz*
(www.poetrysantacruz.org).
Now & then, I write poetry.

I first heard of Wesli Court in Lew Turco's intro to poetry class. He cited Court's work in his own books and pointed them out in others. I gathered Lew probably knew the guy.

One day I was talking to my Logic professor, Dr. Carnes. He broke off on a tangent and mentioned a wonderful poem titled "Dawn Song" someone had written for him, about what it must have been like for the first person — perhaps a caveman — to actually notice the sunrise for more than what it was, to actually see the beauty in it. He showed me the poem in a frame on the wall. I read it and came to the end to find it was written by Wesli Court.

"You know Wesli Court, too? So does Mr. Turco," I said. Dr. Carnes implored me to stare at the name a little longer and see if I did not know him, too.

Then it dawned on me.

Thanks, Lew. I could not have asked for a better teacher. You taught me that the key to everything is learning fundamentals. You shed light on more than just learning poetry.

—Paul Austin

Paul Austin is a 1989 graduate of SUNY Oswego, where he studied Poetry under Lew Turco and won the Georgia Barnes scholarship his senior year. He is now a Software Engineer and Tester at IBM in Poughkeepsie, NY.

A Limerick for Lew

There once was a man named Lew Turco,
for whom prose poetry was loco.
If your poetry in time
did not meter or rhyme,
crudely chime,
bounce a dime,
suck pucker sublime,
or carry at least a hint,
a bare smidgen
(oh yes, I am really pushing it this time)
of metaphorical thyme....
he'd zero you quicker than Zorro!

Ah-hah!

PS: All fun aside, my poetic license hangs in a frame
on the wall and although I am not always sure I
deserve it, I treasure it as much as (if not more
than) all of my other degrees. Although it wasn't
always easy wracking my brain through the icy cold
mazes of amphibrachs, quatrains and something called a
Cyhydedd Hir (which I remember trying to write even
though I could not figure out how to say it aloud),
studying poetry in Turco's form-based boot camp makes
up some of the fondest memories I have of my college
years, circa '91-'93.

Thanks Lew. You're the Greatest!

—JD McDonnell

Lew taught me formal poetry in the mid-seventies, a rich historical time when hippies began to be threatened by persons who admired John Travolta. No one felt safe. No one knew what would happen next — especially in poetry critiques. Critiques were and are the best chance to witness drama, ego destruction and defensive posturing. Lew's critiques were no different.

One especially memorable critique involved Lew Lew (as I was wont to call Mr. Turco from my girlish fondness) and an older student, Big Suck (as I was wont to call Jim T, from my compassionate Buddha nature).

On this particular day, Big Suck had shared his latest piece of tedium with the class and no one knew what the deuce it was about — fishing maybe? Or abortion — or something... Whatever it was about, Lew was not in the mood to guess. He puffed imperiously on his pipe, leaned back in his jaunty denim jacket and kept saying, "I don't get it. Does anybody get it? I don't get it?"

He said this so much that Jim T (Big Suck) completely shed his usual "I'm-older-and-deserve-respect-and-am-equals-with-the-teacher-and-carry-an-oxblood-briefcase" demeanor—and blurted out, "Lew Turco, STOP being purposely dense!"

At that the room froze and all eyes crossed the permafrost to Lew's impassive face. No one knew what would happen next — which if you'll recall was my earlier point.

Patricia Catto teaches Formal Poetry (go figure!), Literature, and Belly Dance at the Kansas City Art Institute where she is Associate Professor of Liberal Arts. (Pcatto@kcai.edu)

A Pantoum for Dr. Lewis Turco,
The Master of Poetic Form

How subtle language is when woven well,
Like silk it teases soft yet runs steel strong;
We wonder how the perfect phrase is held —
We think it pure but written it is wrong.

Like silk it teases soft yet runs steel strong,
Rich metaphor and phrasing to delight;
We think it pure but written it is wrong,
Enough to quit our effort for the night.

Rich metaphor and phrasing to delight,
We see it here and there yet always far,
Enough to quit our effort for the night,
We turn the wheel and search the lonely star.

But when our language finds that gleaming form,
We wonder how the perfect phrase was held,
Yet hold in hand a sparkle newly born —
How subtle language is when woven well.

—Steven E. Swerdfeger

IT WAS DURING MY SENIOR YEAR at the State University of New York at Oswego that I elected to sign up for some courses in creative writing. Little did I realize then how important that decision would be, and how pivotal it would prove in subsequent years.

Yes, it was well-known on campus that Lewis Turco was the most widely-published member of the entire faculty, as well as one of the finest professors. And despite his daunting reputation, all of my initial fears melted when I began taking Lew's workshop during the Fall Semester in 1969.

The procedure was simple enough: place the work one had rendered during the week in the prescribed basket before the day and time due, so that it could be duplicated and read by everyone before the workshop session. Then come to class, to hear and respond to what everyone had shared. As I now reflect on that wonderful year, I realize that there seemed to have been an unspoken contract between Lew and us students, essentially with Lew saying, 'My best for your best.' And perhaps that is one reason why Lew is such a consummate teacher. That unspoken contract established a true commons, wherein an equanimity was extended to all. And it was helpful to see one's work through another's eyes. Lew, of course, was always able to offer discerning suggestions that went to essence of what needed to be done to improve a poem or story.

After class, we would invariably repair to Shaki Patch for more conversation over various libations. It wasn't long before we organized a Writer's Guild, and I soon realized that it was a very real extension of the workshop itself. Under that apprentice model, opportunity was continually offered to assist us in our common love for language and writing. Part of our bond was that we held its rigors and potentials in the highest esteem.

Lew's wonderful and natural sense of humor also helped to establish that informal, first-name basis for both the workshops and Guild gatherings. After it was agreed upon to call our group a Writer's Guild, Lew quipped that we could henceforth feel 'guildy' about that decision. Little did I realize then that Lew had no doubt read all that was worth reading, when I asked him if he had read Antoine de Saint-Exupéry's *The Little Prince.* His response was, "No. I have only just taken them off the car." I also remember the time when Lew came in holding his *Book of Forms* and a larger volume on writing that he had been invited to develop for the State University of New York. He looked at several of us, and quipped, "These books know more than I do." Reflecting on that year today, I realize that the singular bond that united all of us was our love and devotion to language.

During that year, our Writer's Guild was able to host William Stafford's coming to campus. We also held a Poets for Peace reading during the Spring.

Those were the days of the Vietnam War as well as the demagoguery of the now disgraced Spiro Agnew, who in one of his flairs of description castigated members of the Academy, stating that "a spirit of national masochism prevails, encouraged by an effete corps of impudent snobs who characterize themselves as intellectuals." Lew's response was to place a placard very prominently on his office door that proclaimed: HEADQUARTERS—EFFETE CORPS OF IMPUDENT SNOBS.

I also remember visiting Lew & Jean's home. As we waited for dinner, Lew's marvelous and gorgeous black cat Pookah entered the room, deigned to look at us lesser mortals, and then proceeded to jump up on Lew's lap and make itself at home. In its manner and behavior, there was no doubt that this was singularly Lew's cat, a poet's cat, and no mortal being should endeavor to come between them.

During the Spring of 1970 there was enormous upheaval at universities throughout America. At a critical meeting of the college community, I well remember how the meeting's chair, Dr. Kenneth Jones, Vice-Chair of the Faculty Assembly, would invariably recognize Professor Turco and welcome his suggestions, as members of the college sought wisdom on how best to respond to the growing emergencies.

And it was during the Fall of that year — Spring — that Lew was one of the participants in a series of major scholars from various universities throughout the country. I remember that Lew spoke of the poetry of James Dickey, among other things, and at one point during his talk, he stated with knowing conviction, "One thing is certain: we will all be alive forever." When I heard those words, I knew they were true. Although they were true in a way that transcended conventional understandings.

And isn't that what poets do? They successfully transcend the status quo, the norm, the accepted conventions. They continually push us to a keener awareness, wherein we can encounter disarming truths that can awaken our minds and hearts, as well as open doors to transformation.

Lew Turco kindled my love for language and literature. His teaching, his poetry, his scholarship, and his unassuming love for all that language can be and do afforded me a comprehensive foundation for language and writing. It also helped when he would remind us, "A poet is born in his or her twenties." This astute insight gave a long-term perspective that offered new hope and increased confidence.

Thank you, Lew, more than words can say, for all that you have done for me and for countless others. Some make ripples in lakes, and that is enough; your ripples have created enduring waves that continue to help and to inspire generations of writers and scholars.

Steven E. Swerdfeger holds a Ph.D. in creative writing from Union Institute & University. His first novel, *Thursday's Child*, was accorded Finalist Honors in the *1997 Small Press Book Awards*, and will be republished in 2005 under the new title *The Canasta Capers*, together with two companion volumes *An Opening of Heart* and *Because They Think They Can*. His short story "Land and Love" was recently selected as lead story for *Chicken Soup From The Soul of Hawai'i*. In addition to serving as president of Cloudbank Creations and Star Cloud Press, he is a member of the adjunct English faculty at Paradise Valley Community College in Phoenix, Arizona.

Biographical Information About Essayists

HERBERT R. COURSEN, JR. was born in New Jersey and attended Amherst College, where he boxed, and played lacrosse, football, squash, and tennis. He has published nine novels, twenty six books of poetry, and some fifteen critical works. He was a fighter pilot in the USAF in the 1950s and an early opponent of the war in Vietnam. He lives in Maine.

DR. MARY ASWELL DOLL, a former graduate student and colleague of Lewis Turco at S. U. N. Y. College at Oswego, teaches at Savannah College of Art and Design. Formerly Professor of English at Our Lady of Holy Cross College in Louisiana, she is the author of *Like Letters in Running Water, A Mythopoetics of Curriculum, Beckett and Myth: An Archetypal Approach, To the Lighthouse and Back: Writings on Teaching and Living*, and co-editor of *How We Work* and *In the Shadow of the Giant: Thomas Wolfe*.

R. S. GWYNN was born in Eden, North Carolina, in 1948. He attended Davidson College, receiving his B.A. in 1969, after which he did graduate work at the Bread Loaf School of English and entered graduate school at the University of Arkansas, earning the M.A. in 1972 and the M.F.A. in 1973. While a student at Arkansas, he received the John Gould Fletcher Award for Poetry. Gwynn began publishing while an undergraduate, with poetry, fiction, and translations appearing in the *New England Review* and the *Sewanee Review*. His first collection of poetry, *Bearing & Distance*, appeared from Cedar Rock Press in 1977 and was followed by *The Narcissiad*, a satirical poem, in 1982. His book of poems *The Drive-In* won the Breakthrough Award from the University of Missouri Press in 1986. *No Word of Farewell: Poems 1970-2000* was published by Story Line Press in 2000. His poems appear in a number of anthologies and textbooks, including *The Made Thing: Contemporary Southern Poetry, Sound and Sense, Western Wind, Rebel Angels: Twenty-five Poets of the New Formalism*, and *The Book of Forms*. He lives in Beaumont, Texas, with his wife, Donna. They have three sons and one grandchild.

DR. WILLIAM HEYEN, Professor Emeritus of English at S. U. N. Y. College at Brockport, is the author of many books and chapbooks of poetry, the latest being *Diana, Charles, & the Queen* (1997) and editor of, among others, *American Poets* in 1976. He has been a Fulbright lecturer in Germany, the recipient of a Fellowship from the National Endowment in the Arts, and several fellowships of the S. U. N. Y. Foundation. His collection of American poetry is a feature of the Special Collections of the University of Rochester.

DONALD JUSTICE was born in Miami, Florida, in 1925. A graduate of the University of Miami, he attended the universities of North Carolina, Stanford, and Iowa. His books include *New and Selected Poems* (Alfred A. Knopf, 1995); *A Donald Justice Reader* (1991); *The Sunset Maker* (1987), a collection of poems, stories and a memoir; *Selected Poems* (1979), for which he won the Pulitzer Prize; *Departures* (1973); *Night Light* (1967); and *The Summer Anniversaries* (1959), which received the Academy's Lamont Poetry Selection. He has held teaching positions at Syracuse University, the University of California at Irvine, Princeton University, the University of Virginia, and the University of Iowa, and from 1982 until his retirement in 1992, he taught at the University of Florida, Gainesville. He won the Bollingen Prize in Poetry in 1991 and has received grants in poetry from the Guggenheim Foundation, the Rockefeller Foundation, and the National Endowment for the Arts. He served as a Chancellor of The Academy of American Poets from 1997 to 2003. He lives with his wife, Jean Ross, in Iowa City.

DR. DONALD MASTERSON, Associate Professor of English and women's track coach at Oswego State University, took all three of his degrees from the University of Illinois. In 1985 he received a Chancellor's Award for Excellence in Teaching, and he has published in *The Cream City Review*.

DR. DE VILLO SLOAN, who took his B. A. from S.U.N.Y. College at Potsdam and his Ph. D. from S.U.N.Y at Buffalo, has published in *Lake Effect, Sewanee Review*, and *Voices in Italian Americana*. He is Director of the Office of Public Relations at Wells College in Aurora, New York.

Professor Emeritus of English Felix Stefanile taught for many years at Purdue University where he edited and published the long-run and highly regarded poetry periodical *Sparrow*. One of our finest poets of the contemporary period, in 1998 he received the first John Ciardi Award for lifetime achievement in poetry, and in the same year he was the judge for the first annual Bordighera Bi-Lingual Poetry Prize, which he awarded to Lewis Turco.

Gene van Troyer is the former editor of *Star*Lines*, the magazine of the Science Fiction Poetry Society; he has published there and in *The English Record*. For many years he has lived in Japan.

Kathrine Varnes has been reading the words of Emily Dickinson and Lewis Turco for over twenty years. Co-editor with Annie Finch of *An Exaltation of Forms: Contemporary Poets Celebrate the Diversity of Their Work* (Michigan UP, 2002), Varnes has published essays primarily on feminism, prosody, and contemporary poetry. Word Tech Editions will publish her book of poems *The Paragon*, which contains a long poem using the words of Herbert Marcuse's "Essay on Liberation," in January 2005.

The late Dr. Hyatt H. Waggoner of Brown University was one of the most highly respected scholars of the American literature of the nineteenth century. His book, *American Poetry from the Puritans to the Present* is the standard history of the subject, and he has written and edited books and articles on Hawthorne, Whittier, and many others.

The late Gerhard Zeller was associate professor of English at S.U.N.Y. Oswego. He published posthumously in *E. L. F., Eclectic Literary Forum*.

A BIBLIOGRAPHY OF REVIEWS OF THE WORK OF
LEWIS TURCO

I. *Day After History: A Selection of Poems*, Arlington: Privately circulated, 1956. Criticism of the volume, or of poems appearing in it:
A. "Foreword" to reprint edition of *Day After History*, by Lewis Turco, [op. cit.], Ann Arbor: University Microfilms O-P Books, 1967.
II. *First Poems*, Francestown: Golden Quill Press, 1960.
Criticism of the volume, or of poems appearing in it:
A. "Foreword" by Stanley Romaine Hopper to *Riverside Poetry 3*, edited by Marianne Moore, Howard Nemerov, and Alan Swallow, New York: Twayne, 1958.
B. "Foreword" to *First Poems*, op. cit., by Donald Justice.
C. *Meriden Journal* (Connecticut), Jul. 13, 1960, unsigned article and interview.
D. *Morning Record* (Connecticut), Wed., Jul. 20, 1960, review by Lydia B. Atkinson.
E. *American Weave*, Autumn 1960, review by Donald Justice [same as II.B.].
F. *Iowa Defender* (Iowa City), iii:3, Mon., Oct. 10, 1960, "A Perceptive Romantic," by Gregory FitzGerald.
G. *Miami Herald* (Florida), Sun., Oct. 23, 1960, review by Hannah Kahn.
H. *The Sunday Star* (Washington, DC,), Dec. 4, 1960, review by Richard Eberhart.
I. *Hudson Review*, Winter 1960-61, "A Catalogue of Poets," by John Thompson.
J. *Voices*, No. 174, Jan.-Apr., 1961, "Cerebral Modernists," by Conrad Pendleton.
K. *The Capital Times* (Madison, WI), Thur. Apr. 27, 1961, review by August Derleth.
L. *Sewanee Review*, lxix:2, Spring 1961, "The Death and Keys of the Censor," by James Dickey.
M. *La Luce* (Italy), liv:17, 10 Sep. 1961, unsigned review.
N. *Abstracts of English Studies*, iv:10, Oct. 1961.
O. *Poetry*, xcix:3, Dec., 1961, "Four First Volumes," by Philip Legler.

P. *Prairie Schooner,* xxxvi: 3, Fall 1962, "Dialogue in Limbo," by Robert P. Dana.

Q. Dickey, James, *Babel to Byzantium,* New York: Farrar, Straus and Giroux, 1968, p. 141 [same as II.E.].

R. *Modern Poetry Studies,* ii:3, 1971, "The Progress of Lewis Turco" by William Heyen.

S. *DeKalb Literary Arts Journal,* v:2, 1971, [same as II.R].

T. Ross, Jean W., ed., *Dictionary of Literary Biography Yearbook: 1984,* Detroit: Gale Research, 1985, "Lewis Turco," by Mary Doll, pp. 331-338.

III. *The Sketches of Lewis Turco and Livevil: A Mask,* Cleveland: American Weave Press, 1962.
Criticism of the volume, or of poems appearing in it:
A. "Introduction" to *The Sketches,* (op. cit.) by Loring Williams.
B. *Poetry,* cii:6, Sep. 1963, "Five Poets," by John Engels, pp. 402-405.
C. *Voices — A Journal of Poetry,* no. 184, May-Aug. 1964, "The Gift and the Variety," by Archibald Henderson, pp. 43-45.
D. *Quartet,* No. 3, Spring 1963, "Review" by James L. Allen, Jr.

IV. *Awaken, Bells Falling: Poems 1959-1967,* Columbia: University of Missouri Press, 1968.
Criticism of the volume, or of poems appearing in it:
A. See II.R. above.
B. *Virginia Quarterly Review,* xliv: 4, Autumn 1968, unsigned review by R. H. W. Dillard.
C. *Poetry,* cxiii:6, Mar. 1969, "Books That Look Out, Books That Look In," by William Stafford, pp. 421-425.
D. *Concerning Poetry,* ii:2, Fall 1969, "The Formalism of Lewis Turco: Fluting and Fifing with Frosted Fingers," by Hyatt H. Waggoner, pp. 50-58.
E. *Northwest Review,* x:13, Summer 1970, "Three Poets," by Henry Carlile, pp. 124-128.
F *DeKalb Literary Arts Journal,* iv:4, 1970, "Craft and Vision: An Interview with Lewis Turco," edited by David G. McLean, pp. 1-14.

G. *American Weave*, No. 33, 1971, "Three Reviews," by Mary Oliver, pp. 61-67.

H. *Vermont Freeman*, Early November 1971, "Checkers or Chess" by Terry Stanion, p. 9.

I. *Costerus: Essays in English and American Language and Literature* (Netherlands), Vol. 9, 1973, "The Poetry of Lewis Turco," an interview by Gregory Fitz Gerald and William Heyen.

J. James F. Mersman, *Out of the Vietnam Vortex*, Lawrence: University Press of Kansas, 1974, p. 214.

K. Dedria Bryfonski, ed., *Contemporary Literary Criticism*, Vol. 11, Detroit: Gale Research, 1979, "Lewis Turco" entry quoting from II.R., IV.B., IV.I., IX.A., XI.C.

L. See II.T. above.

V. *The Book of Forms: A Handbook of Poetics*, New York: E. P. Dutton, 1968.

Criticism of the volume:

A. *Palladium-Times* (Oswego NY), 1968, review by Frank Hulme.

B. See XVI.C. below.

VI. *The Inhabitant*, Northampton: Despa Press, 1970.

Criticism of the volume, or of poems appearing in it:

A. *Kamadhenu*, ii:1 & 2, 1971, review by Kelsie Harder.

B. *December*, xiii:1-2, 1971, review by Dave Etter.

C. *Maine Times* (Brunswick), l:3, Sep. 17, 1971, "Human House" by Herb Coursen [short version of VI.G.].

D. *Massachusetts Review*, xii:4, Fall 1971, review by Josephine Miles, pp. 700-702.

E. *Agora*, ii:1, Spring 1972, review by David G. McLean.

F. See II.R. above.

G. *Bartleby's Review*, i:1, Fall 1972, "A Certain Slant of Light," by Herbert R. Coursen, Jr., pp. 39-43.

H. *Poetry*, cxxi:6, Mar. 1973, review by Jonathan Galassi, pp. 344-348.

I. See II.T. above.

J. See IV.K. above.

K. See XXV.Q. below.

VII. *The Literature of New York: A Selective Bibliography of Colonial and Native New York State Authors*, Oneonta: New York State English Council, 1970.

VIII. *Creative Writing in Poetry*, Albany: State University of New York, 1970.

IX. *Pocoangelini: A Fantography and Other Poems*, Northampton: Despa Press, 1971.
Criticism of the volume, or of poems appearing in it:
A. *Italian Americana*, i:2, Spring 1975, review by Felix Stefanile.
B. See IV.K. above.
C. See II.T. above.
D. See XXV.K. below.

X. *Freshman Composition and Literature*, Albany: State University of New York, 1973.

XI. *The Weed Garden*, Orangeburg: Peaceweed Press, 1973.
Criticism of the volume, or of poems appearing in it:
A. *Mississippi Review*, 1974, review by H. A. Maxson, pp. 101-103.
B. *Modern Poetry Studies*, v:3, Winter 1974, "Lewis Turco's Best Book of Poems," by Roger Dickinson-Brown, pp. 286-89.
C. See IV.E. above.
D. See IV.K. above.
E. See II.T. above.
F. See XXV.Q. below.

XII. *Poetry: An Introduction Through Writing*, Reston: Reston Publishing Co., 1973.
Criticism of the volume:
A. *Bardic Echoes*, xiv:1, March 1973, unsigned review.
B. *English Record*, Fall 1973, review by Robert F. Saunders, pp. 69-70.
C. Phillis Gershator, comp., *A Bibliographic Guide to the Literature of Contemporary American Poetry*, 1970-1975, Metuchen: The Scarecrow Press, 1976, unsigned review, p. 96.

D. *Star * Line*, vii:1, Jan./Feb. 1984, review by Gene Van Troyer.
E. See XXV.T. below.

XIII. *Courses in Lambents: Poems by Wesli Court*, Oswego: Mathom Publishing Co., 1977.
Criticism of the volume, or of poems appearing in it:
A. *Sam Houston Literary Review*, iii:1, Apr. 1978, review by Keith Cameron, p. 82.

XIV. *Curses and Laments by Wesli Court*, Stevens Point: Song, No. 5, 1978.

XV. *Murgatroyd and Mabel by Wesli Court*, Oswego: Mathom Publishing Co., 1978.
Criticism of the volume:
A. *Palladium-Times* (Oswego NY), Thu. Dec. 14, 1978, review by Rosemary S. Nesbitt, p. 14.

XVI. *A Cage of Creatures*, Potsdam: Banjo Press, 1978.
Criticism of the volume, or of poems appearing in it:
A. *Star * Line*, v:4, Jul./Aug. 1982, review by Gene Van Troyer, pp. 6-8.
B. *Sunday Patriot-News* (Harrisburg PA), March 7, 1982, review by George Myers, Jr., p. 24.
C. *Cream City Review*, viii:1 & 2, 1983, "Making the Language Dance and Go Deep: An Interview with Lewis Turco," by Donald Masterson, ed. Jack Welch, pp. 108-117.
D. See XXV.K. below.
E. See XXV.Q. below.
F. See XXV.T. below.

XVII. *Seasons of the Blood*, Rochester: Mammoth Press, 1980.
Criticism of the volume, or of poems appearing in it:
A. *Portland Review* (Oregon), xxviii:1, 1980, unsigned review.
B. *Star * Line*, v:1, Jan.-Feb. 1982, review by Gene Van Troyer, pp. 6-7.
C. See II.T. above.

D.   See XVI.B. above.
E.   See XXV.T. below.

XVIII. *American Still Lifes*, Oswego: Mathom Publishing Co, 1981.
Criticism of the volume, or of poems appearing in it:
A.   "Introduction" to the volume by H. R. Coursen, pp. 4-6.
B.   See II.T. above.
C.   See XVI.B. above.
D.   *Star*Line*, "Passing in Review" by Gene Van Troyer, vi:4,
July/August 1983, pp. 21-23.
E.   See XXV.K. below.
F.   See XXV.Q. below.
G.   "A Chance to Chat with a Poet" by Warren F. Gardner, *The
Record* (Meriden, Connecticut), 24 March 1992, Op-Ed page.

XIX.   *The Airs of Wales* by Wesli Court, Philadelphia: Temple
University *Poetry Newsletter*, No. 53, Fall 1981.

XX. *The Compleat Melancholick*, Minneapolis: The Bieler Press, 1985.
Criticism of the volume, or of poems appearing in it:
A.   *Record-Journal* (Meriden CT), Sun. Jun. 9, 1985, review by Don
Aucoin, pp. C-1 & C-3.
B.   *Choice*, Oct. 1985, review by D. A. Barton.
C.   *Lake Effect*, i:3, Special Holiday Issue 1986, review by Victoria B.
Cooley.
D.   *The Fessenden Review*, x:4, 1986, unsigned review.
E.   *The Hollins Critic*, xxiii:5, Dec. 1986, review by Hyatt H.
Waggoner.
F.   See II.T. above.
G.   See XXV.K. below.

XXI. *Visions and Revisions of American Poetry*, Fayetteville: University
of Arkansas Press, 1986.
Criticism of the volume:
A.   *Arkansas Democrat*, Oct. 26, 1986, unsigned review.
B.   *Choice*, Nov. 1986, review by P. Smith, p. 180.
C.   *Booklist*, January 1, 1987, review by Penelope Mesick.

D. *Kliatt Young Adult Paperbook Guide*, January 1987, review by Morris Rabinowitz.

E. *American Literature*, Mar. 1987, review by Margaret Dickie.

F. *Centennial Review*, xxxi:2, Spring 1987, Review by Diane Wakoski.

G. *Times Literary Supplement* (London), May 22, 1987, "Jocks and Jockeying," by Mark Ford, p. 557.

H. *Journal of Modern Literature*, Summer 1987, review by "S.A.S."

I. *Book Review Digest*, lxxxiii:9, 1987, quotes from XXI.B., E., & G. above.

J. *The Hollins Critic*, xxv:5, December 1988, review by Alfred Dorn.

K. *The Year's Work in English Studies*, Vol. 67 for 1986, London: The English Association/John Murray, 1989.

L. *Voices in Italian Americana*, i:2, Fall 1990, review by Elizabeth Blair, pp. 152-3.

XXII. *The New Book of Forms: A Handbook of Poetics*, Hanover: University Press of New England, 1986.
Criticism of the volume:

A. *Post-Standard* (Syracuse), Aug. 5, 1986, article by Russell Tarby.

B. *Maine Sunday Telegram*, Sep. 7, 1986, article by Kendall Merriam, p. 5A.

C. *Palladium-Times* (Oswego), Oct. 21, 1986, unsigned article.

D. *Booklist*, Jan. 1, 1987, review by "P. M."

E. *Young Adult Paperbook Guide*, Jan. 1987, review by "M. R."

F. *Arts Letter* (Vermont Council on the Arts), Mar./Apr. 1987, review by Geof Hewitt.

G. *Virginia Quarterly Review*, lxiii:2, Spring 1987, unsigned review.

H. *Fessenden Review*, xi:4, 1987, unsigned review.

I. *Choice*, Sep. 1987, review by C. L. Snyder, p. 213.

J. *Eidos*, iv:2, Dec. 1987, review by Sally Gall.

K. *Sewanee Review*, xcvi:1, Jan.-Mar. 1988, "Forms of Poetry," by Stephen Cushman.

L. *Rocky Mountain Review*, Spring 1988, review by Tom Trusky.

M. *American Poetry*, v:2, Winter 1988, unsigned review.

N. *Pen Points*, The Newsletter of the Philadelphia Writers' Conference, Inc., Winter 1992, unsigned review.

O. See XXV.T. below.

P.   Review by R. T. Smith, on the Internet, 1999.

XXIII. *A Maze of Monsters*, Livingston: Livingston University Press, 1986.
Criticism of the volume, or of poems appearing in it:
A.   *The News*, (State University of New York), April 1987, unsigned review.
B.   See XVI.C. above.
C.   See XXV.K. below.
D.   See XXV.Q. below.
E.   *Poetry Pilot*, November-December 1991, "What Is Italian-American Poetry?" by Dana Gioia, pp. 3-10.
F.   See XXV.T. below.

XXIV. *Dialogue, Cincinnati: Writer's Digest Books*, 1989.
Criticism of the volume:
A.   *Romance Writer's Report*, May, 1989, review by Sandy Huseby, p. 53.
B.   *The Palladium-Times*, (Oswego, N. Y.), Thursday, June 8, 1989.
C.   *The Valley News*, (Fulton, N. Y.), Monday, June 12, 1989.
D.   *Bookwatch*, Vol. 10, July 1989, p. 7.
E.   *Record-Journal*, (Meriden, CT), Sunday, August 13, 1989, p. E-8.
F.   *Authorship*, National Writers Club, Summer 1989, "Books for Writers," by Sandra Whelchel, p. 4.
G.   *SPWAO Newsletter*, xi:4, July/August 1989, review by Audrey Parente, p. 15.
H.   *Fort Fairfield Review*, Wednesday, Sept. 6, 1989, "View from Northridge" column by Marnie Higgins, p. 14.
I.   *Tarc Report*, Nov.-Dec. 1989.
J.   *Community College Journalist*, Fall 1989, review by Anna M. Ingalls, pp. 18-19.
K.   *Sewanee Review*, xcviii:3, Summer 1990, "American Publishing Today" by George Garrett, p. 525.
L.   *Freelance Writer's Report*, ix:10, December 1990, p. 8.
M.   *Maine in Print*, August 1991, "Tools of the Trade," by Kurtis Clements, p. 11.
N.   *Lake Effect*, vi:3, Fall 1991, review by Rex Derby, pp. 17- 18.

O. *Voices in Italian Americana*, iii:2, 1992, review by Patricia Hart, pp. 143-144.

XXV. *The Shifting Web: New and Selected Poems*, Fayetteville: University of Arkansas Press, 1989.
Criticism of the volume or of poems appearing in it:
A. *Record-Journal* (Meriden, CT), Tuesday, September 12, 1989, p. 6.
B. *Campus Update*, (SUNY Oswego), i:2, September 13, 1989.
C. *The Palladium-Times* (Oswego NY), Thursday, September 14, 1989, p. 6 of the "Preview" section.
D. *The Valley News* (Fulton NY), Thursday, September 14, 1989.
E. *Booklist*, October 15, 1989, review by Jim Elledge.
F. Ibid., review by Hazel Rochman.
G. *The News*, State University of New York, Fall 1989.
H. *Library Journal*, Nov. 6, 1989, review by Louis McKee.
I. *This Month in Maine Literature*, iv:11, December 1989/January 1990, review by Herbert Coursen.
J. *University Press Book News*, December 1989, p. 24.
K. *Poetry Pilot*, Academy of American Poets, February 1990, "Books Noted," p. 12.
L. *Lake Effect*, v:1, Spring 1990, review by De Villo Sloan, pp. 21-22.
M. *Choice*, April 1990, review by B. Wallenstein, p. 216.
N. *Voices in Italian Americana*, I:1, Spring 1990, review by Elizabeth Blair, pp. 186-89.
O. *Dictionary of Literary Biography Yearbook: 1989*, Detroit: Gale Research, 1990, "The Year in Poetry" by R. S. Gwynn, pp. 60-61.
P. See XXVI.A. below.
Q. *The Hollins Critic*, xxviii:2, April, 1991, "A Certain Slant of Light: The Poetry of Lewis Turco," by Herbert R. Coursen, Jr., pp. 1-10. See V.6, XVIII.A, and XXV.I. above.
R. See XXIII.E. above.
S. *Sewanee Review*, xcix:4, Fall 1991, "A Capacity for Song" by De Villo Sloan (same as L. above), pp. cx-cxii.
T. *The English Record*, xlii:2, 1992, "Terra Imaginaria" by Gene Van Troyer, pp. 11-18. See XII.D, XVI.A., and XVII.B. above.
U. *Voices in Italian Americana*, "The Mirror Image: A Retrospective View of Lewis Turco," by De Villo Sloan, iii:1, Spring 1992.

XXVI. *A Family Album*, Eugene: Silverfish Review, 1990.
Criticism of the volume or of poems appearing in it:
A. Syracuse, N. Y., *Herald-American* Accent: Oswego County, 4 July 1990, "Prof Has Verbal Feistiness, Poetic Skill," by Scott Scanlon.
B. *The Oswegonian*, lvi:7, October 25, 1990, Arts & Entertainment section, "Turco to Tell Tales in Poetry," by George Liveris.
C. *Maine in Print* (formerly *This Month in Maine Literature*), v:10, November 1990, review by Herb R. Coursen, p. 5.
D. *Lake Effect*, v:4, Winter 1991, review by Barbara Adams.
E. *The Georgia Review*, xlv:4, Winter 1991, "A Traveler among Mockingbirds," by Ted Kooser, pp. 792-803.
F. *Voices in Italian Americana*, iv:1, Spring 1993, review by Diane Raptosh, pp. 217-219.
G. See also XXVIII.C. below.

XXVII. *The Public Poet*, Ashland: Ashland Poetry Press, 1991.
Criticism of the volume:
A. "Foreword" to *The Public Poet*, op. cit., by Robert McGovern, pp. iv-v.
B. *The Palladium-Times* (Oswego), Thursday, April 4, 1991, "Turco returns from Ohio...."
C. *Emily Dickinson International Society Bulletin*, v:2, Nov./Dec. 1993, "Recent & Forthcoming," p. 12.

XXVIII. *Murmurs in the Walls*, El Reno: Cooper House, 1992.
Criticism of the volume or of poems appearing in it:
A. *Poet*, ii:4, Winter 1990-91, pp. 10-11, "The Annual Chapbook Competition," pp. 10-11.
B. *Campus Update* (SUNYCO), iii:17, June 17, 1992, pp. 2-3.
C. *The New Review*, i:2, Sep.-Oct. 1992, "Ghosts of Blinn's Hill" by Herbert R. Coursen, Jr., pp. 48-49.
D. *Dusty Dog Reviews*, nos. 10 & 11, May 10, 1993, p. 42.
E. *The Bridge*, iii:2, Summer - Fall 1993, Review by Gertrude M. White, pp. 183-186.

XXIX. *Emily Dickinson: Woman of Letters*, Albany: State University of New York Press, 1993.

Criticism of the volume or of poems appearing in it:

A. *Emily Dickinson International Society Bulletin*, v:1, May/June 1993, review by Sarah Wider, pp. 11-12.

B. *Campus Update*, iv:17, June 16, 1993, "Book Inspired by Dickinson" by Michele Reed, pp. 2-3.

C. *The Bookwatch*, September 1993, "The Literary Shelf," September 1993, p. 11.

D. *Reference and Research Book News*, viii:7, Nov. 1993.

E. *Nineteenth-Century Literature*, il:1, June 1994, review by Willis Buckingham, pp. 538-543.

F. *E.L.F: Eclectic Literary Forum*, v:3, Fall 1995, "The Place of Reputation" by Kevin Walzer, pp. 50-51.

XXX. *Legends of the Mists*, Kew Gardens: New Spirit Press, 1993.
Criticism of the volume or of poems appearing in it:
A. Dusty Dog Reviews, Nos. 14/15, 1994.

XXXI. *How to Write a Million* (with Ansen Dibell and Orson Scott Card), London: Robinson Publishing, 1995.
Criticism of the volume, or of stories appearing in it:
A. *Campus Update*, April 3, 1996, "Turco Co-Author of U. K. Book," by Michele Reed, p. 2.

XXXII. *Bordello, Poems, and Prints by George O'Connell*, Oswego: Grey Heron Press, 1996.
Criticism of the volume, or of poems appearing in it:
A. *Spectrum A Review of the Arts & Cultures of Oswego County*, iv:2, March 1996, "Bordello, a Creative Unity of Visual and Literary Art," p. 3.

XXXIII. *Shaking the Family Tree, A Remembrance*, West Lafayette: Bordighera, 1998.
Criticism of the volume or of material appearing in it:
A. *The Syracuse New Times*, "Italian Yankee" by Russell Tarby, No 1436, Oct. 7-14, 1998, pp. 12-13.
B. *The Kennebec (Maine) Journal*, Sunday, January 24, 1999, p. D5.

C. Review by Martha King on www.italians-world.org/altreitalie/19 Libri7.htm.

XXXIV. *A Book of Fears*, translated into Italian by Joseph Alessia, West Lafayette: Bordighera, 1998.
Criticism of the volume or of poems appearing in it:
A. See A.XXXIII, above.
B. See B.XXXIII, above.
C. "Preface" to *A Book of Fears*, op. cit. by Felix Stefanile.
D. Fra Noi, Chicagoland's Italian American Voice, "The Many Faces of Fear" by Fred L. Gardaphé, 37:12, December 1998.
E. *Kirkus Reviews*, November 15, 1998, unsigned review (on the Internet).
F. *A(merican) I(talian) H(istorical) A(ssociation) Newsletter*, review by Hal Sirowitz, Vol. 32, No. 3 & 4, 1999, p. 7.
G. *Testo a Fronte, Semestrale di Teoria e Pratica Della Traduzione Letteraria*, review by Franco Buffoni, Numero 21, II Semestre 1999, p. 284.

XXV. *The Book of Literary Terms, The Genres of Fiction, Drama, Nonfiction, Literary Criticism and Scholarship*, Hanover: University Press of New England, 1999.
Criticism of the volume:
A. *Choice*, June 2000, review by R. H. McDonald.
B. *M.W. P. A. Maine in Print*, March/April 2002, "Member News,"

XXVI. *The Book of Forms*, Third Edition, Hanover: University Press of New England, 2000.
Criticism of the volume:

XXVII. *The Green Maces of Autumn, Voices in an Old Maine House*, Dresden: The Mathom Bookshop, 2002
Criticism of the Volume:
A. "Foreword" to *The Green Maces of Autumn*, op. cit., by Herbert R. Coursen. (See "Ghosts of Blinn's Hill" by Herbert R. Coursen, Jr., The New Review, i:2, Sep.-Oct. 1992, pp. 48-49).
B. See also XXVI. A.-G. above.

C. See also XXVIII, A.-E. above.

D. *Portland Sunday Telegram*, Sunday, August 18th, 2002, "Recently Published," Audience section mention.

E. *Bangor Daily News*, Monday, August 26, 2002, "Turco Uses Past Voices to Share New Poetry," review by Carl Little, pp. C6-7.

GENERAL REFERENCES AND BIBLIOGRAPHIES

Ferdinando P. Alfonsi, *Dictionary of Italian-American Poets*, Bern: Peter Lang, 1989, pp. 153-156.

Marilyn K. Basel, "Lewis (Putnam) Turco, ('Wesli Court')," *Contemporary Authors, New Revision Series*, vol. 24, ed. Straub, Detroit: Gale Research, 1988.

Dedria Bryfonski, ed., *Contemporary Literary Criticism*, Vol. 11, Detroit: Gale Research, 1979, "Lewis Turco" entry quoting from II.R., IV.B., IV.I., VIII.A., X.B., pp. 549-552.

Tracy Chevalier, ed., *Contemporary Poets*, 5th edition, Chicago and London: St. James Press, 1991, entry by Jim Elledge, q.v., pp. 996-999.

Herbert R. Coursen, Jr., "A Certain Slant of Light: The Poetry of Lewis Turco," *The Hollins Critic*, xxviii:2, April, 1991, pp. 1-10.

— , reprint, *Companion to Contemporary American Literature from the Editors of The Hollins Critic*, ed. R. H. W. Dillard and Amanda Cockrell, Farmington Hills: Twayne Publishers, 2002.

Mary Doll, "Lewis Turco," *Dictionary of Literary Biography Yearbook: 1984*, ed. Ross, Detroit: Gale Research, 1985.

Jim Elledge, "Lewis Turco," *Contemporary Poets*, 4th ed., Vinson, London: St. James, & New York: St. Martin's, 1985.

— , ibid., 5th ed., Chevalier, London & Chicago: St. James, 1991. [Update of previous entry.]

— , ibid., 6th ed., Chevalier, London & Chicago: St. James, 1996. [Update of previous entry.]

Gregory Fitz Gerald, and William Heyen, "The Poetry of Lewis Turco," an interview, *Costerus: Essays in English and American Language and Literature* (Netherlands), Vol. 9, 1973.

F. W. Crumb Memorial Library, eds., *Bibliographies in Contemporary Poetry*, "Lewis Turco: A Bibliography of His Works and Criticism of Them," Potsdam: State University of New York College, 1972.

Phillis Gershator, ed., *A Bibliographic Guide to the Literature of Contemporary American Poetry, 1970-75*, Metuchen: Scarecrow, 1976.

Martin E. Gingerich, comp., *Contemporary Poetry in America and England 1950-1975: A Guide to Information Sources*, Detroit: Gale Research, 1983, pp. 393-394.

R. S. Gwynn, "Lewis Putnam Turco," *Encyclopedia of American Literature*, ed. Steven R. Serafin, New York: Continuum, 1999, pp. 1161-2.

William Heyen, "Lewis Turco," *Contemporary Poets*, ed. Vinson, idem., 2nd ed., New York: St. Martin's Press, 1975, pp. 1570-1572.

— , ibid., 3rd ed., New York: St. Martin's Press, 1980.[Update of previous entry.]

— , "The Progress of Lewis Turco," *Modern Poetry Studies*, ii:3, 1971.

Frank. N. Magill, ed., *Critical Survey of Short Fiction*, Englewood Cliffs: Salem Press, 1981, p. 2861.

Jerre Mangione & Ben Morreale, *La Storia: Five Centuries of the Italian Experience*, New York: HarperCollins, 1992, pp. 430-434.

Donald Masterson,, "Making the Language Dance and Go Deep: An Interview with Lewis Turco," ed. Jack Welch, *Cream City Review*, viii:1 & 2, 1983, pp. 108-117.

Roger Matuz, ed., *Contemporary Literary Criticism*, Vol. 63, Detroit: Gale Research, 1991, "Lewis Turco" entry quoting from II.O., IV.C., IV.D., IV.I., XXI.E., XXI.F., XXI.G., XXI.J., XXII.C., XXII.D., pp. 428-433.

William McPherson, comp., *The Bibliography of Contemporary American Poetry, 1945-1985: An Annotated Checklist*, Meckler Publishing, 1986, p. 69.

Rosalie Murphy, ed., *Contemporary Poets of the English Language*, Chicago: St. James Press, 1970, pp. 1105-1106.

Jean W. Ross, ed., *Dictionary of Literary Biography Yearbook: 1984*, Detroit: Gale Research, 1985, entry by Mary Doll (with bibliography), pp. 331-338.

De Villo Sloan,, "The Mirror Image: A Retrospective View of Lewis Turco," *Voices in Italian Americana*, iii:1, Spring 1992.

Deborah A. Straub, ed., *Contemporary Authors, New Revision Series*, Vol. 24, Detroit: Gale Research, 1988, entry by Marilyn K. Basel (with bibliography), pp. 446-448.

Lewis Turco, comp., *The Literature of New York: A Selective Bibliography of Colonial and Native New York State Authors*, Oneonta: New York State English Council, 1970, p. 95.

Gene Van Troyer, "Terra Imaginaria," *The English Record*, xlii:2, 1992, pp. 11-18.

James Vinson, ed., *Contemporary Poets*, Second Edition [see Murphy, above], New York: St. Martin's Press, 1975, pp. 1570-1572. [Quotes from II.R. above.]

— , ibid., Third Edition, New York: St. Martin's Press, 1980. [Updates previous entry.]

— , and D. L. Kirkpatrick, eds., ibid., Fourth Edition, 1985. Critical entry by Jim Elledge, q.v.

Hyatt H. Waggoner, "The Formalism of Lewis Turco: Fluting and Fifing with Frosted Fingers," *Concerning Poetry*, ii:2, Fall 1969, pp. 50-58.

Gerhard Zeller, "The Anachronist" (an interview with "Wesli Court") in *E.L.F.: Eclectic Literary Forum*, viii:1, Spring 1998.

Short listings: *Who's Who in America, Lincoln Library of Language Arts, Contemporary Authors, Directory of American Scholars, Directory of American Poets and Fiction Writers, The Writer's Directory, Who's Who in U.S. Writers, Editors, & Poets*, etc.

INDEX

Bradbury, Ray, 43, 44
Bradstreet, Anne, 10
Bread Loaf Writers Conference, 13
breath pause, 67
Brinnin, John Malcolm, 102
Brooklyn Eagle, The, 70
Brooks, Cleanth,
    Modern Poetry and the
    Tradition on Frost, 99
Bryant, William Cullen,
    "Thanatopsis," 73
Buber, Martin, 95, 96
Bunner, Henry Cuyler, 41
"Burning Bush, The," 84
"Burning the News," 87, 88, 91,
    102
Burton, Robert,
    "Compleat Melancholick,
    The," 96, 97

-C-
Cabot, Caboto (the original Italian
    family name of the Cabots), 8
Cage of Creatures, A, 73, 74, 130,
    134, 163, 221
Carleton Miscellany, The, 89
Carlile, Henry, 43, 218
Carnes, Robert, 36, 207
Casagrande, David A.,
    "Rubliw for Lewis Turco," 34
"Cat, The," 108, 112
"Chant of Seasons," 45
Chaucer, Geoffrey, 137
"Chimera," 130
"Church, The," 121
Ciardi, John, 4, 49, 130
    Alphabestiary, An, 130

"Circles," 95
"City's Masque, The," 9
Clementi, Muzio, 42, 44
"Colony, The," 119
Compleat Melancholick, The, 4,
    96, 97, 222
"Compleat Melancholick, The,"
    97
Confessional poetry, 75, 82
Connecticut, University of, 9
"Correspondence," 135
"Couch, The," 103, 109, 110,
    112
Coursen, Herbert R., Jr., 78
    "Whole Meaning Again," Ack.,
    111, 214, 219, 225, 226, 228
Court, Wesli, 4, 17, 43, 44, 49, 64,
    78, 136, 137, 144, 199, 207,
    221, 222, 229, 232
    Courses in Lambents, 44, 136,
    138, 141, 149, 221
    Curses and Laments, 44, 137,
    145, 147, 150, 221
    Murgatroyd and Mabel, 4, 221
Coxe, Louis O., 126
"Craft and Vision," McLean,
    David G., 102, 218, 219
Crane, Stephen,
    "Open Boat, The," 107
Creeley, Robert, 76, 155, 191
Cummings, E. E., 73
"Cups," 134
cyrch a chwta, 11

-D-
Dante, 4, 89, 95
"Death," 178

234

www.ingramcontent.com/pod-product-compliance
Lightning Source LLC
Chambersburg PA
CBHW030940150426

42812CB00064B/3076/J